Magijutsu:

Black & White Egyptian Counter Magic

Magijutsu:

Black & White Egyptian Counter Magic

Horus Michael

Magijutsu®: Black & White Egyptian Counter Magic. Copyright ©® 2020 Horus Michael, All rights reserved.

No part of this work may be reproduced, stored in a retrieval system, or transmitted in any form or by any means, electronic, mechanical, photocopying, recording, or otherwise, without the prior written permission of the Author or Copyright owner.

This book was printed in the U.S.A.

www.amazon.com/author/michaeljcosta

www.amazon.com/author/horusmichael

Genre: Mind, Body & Spirit; Egyptian Magic/Mythology; Occult.

Hieroglyphic Font by Inscribe. **(6x9).**

10 9 8 7 6 5 4 3 2 1

(*This book contains* **excerpts** *from other books* **by the Author.**)

Contents:

Foreword: page 6 – Words of Caution

Chapter 1: page 8 – Misc. Concepts

Chapter 2: page 28 – Magijutsu

Chapter 3: page 44 – Magical First Aid

Chapter 4: page 85 – Protection Spells

Chapter 5: page 100 – Self-Defense

Chapter 6: page 119 – Counter-Magic

Chapter 7: page 149 – Counter-Offensive

Chapter 8: page 203 – Counter-Politics

Chapter 9: page 245 – Offerings, Hymns

Bibliography: page 266

About the Author: page 270

For Professor Glynn Custred, Ph.D. (CSUEB).

Foreword:

Some words of Caution:

Ancient Egyptian Magic uses certain Words of Power in the form of Deity or Spirit Names; that when uttered or written can unleash great powers or effects. This is not a toy to the novice. Simply reading a few words is not a trifling concept – words for Natural Disasters are not simply words in a given language, but a codex that causes events amplified by Carbon Pollution in the atmosphere. Of course, Climate Change has no effect on Cosmic Forces or Earth movements; using this system of Egyptian Magic can cause destruction to an enemy, and bountiful attractions to others.

Evidence for Egyptian Deities is simple: wake one up and watch the effects! Disbelief in the Supernatural is a common fallacy in Modern Eyes. **The author has no responsibility should the reader misuse** this or any books on the subject. **Use this at your own risk!**

Chapter 1: Misc. Concepts

Protection & Offering Hymn

"*An adoration of* **Ptah**, *Lord of Ma'at, Grand Architect of the Universe, who hears prayers of the devoted, the Master Craftsman who created people like Khnum on his potter's wheel. O Ptah, who opens the Mouth of the Spirits above, who opened the Mouth of the Horizon within NWT to release Ra into the daylight, beloved of Nefertum and Imhotep,* **protect** *those who use this book* **from** *hostility and negative energy.*

"*I offer unto* **Ptah the Creator** *of all Life these* **invocation-offerings** *presented in his Marble Temples daily in Men-nefer: May you accept this offering on my behalf, and unto my benefit, of Fresh breads and cakes, Beer and Ale, wine of all kinds, Cooked Meat, fruits and vegetables; royal linen clothing, a mile of farmland with 1000 Ushabtis workers, alabaster vessels, pure water from the deepest part of the river, and a fully-furnished Palace in Men-nefer. May you accept this offering in my name of Pharaoh (***Horus Michael I***); Maahru.*"

(Offering):

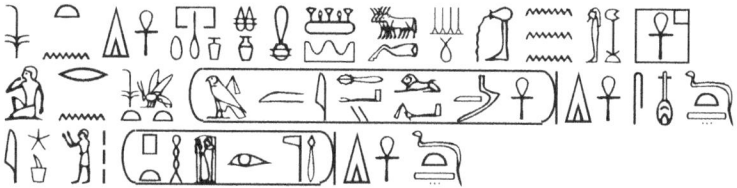

Energy:

Magical or Psychic Energy enables the Spells in this book to work. This energy can be naturally-occurring as in the Tropics or places close to Ra, the Sun, like in an airplane or space shuttle. The energy can also be generated by actions, or summoned to you with an attraction spell. It may be Bio-rhythmic, a pattern of one's spiritual and mental energy per month. Energy is also bestowed by benevolence of the Egyptian Gods, as in Good Luck (**Lux**) for performing positive actions or deeds like righteous conduct or **upholding Ma'at** in society.

White Magic is beneficial to your city, family, home, or self. It is positive Magical effect. **Black Magic** is beneficial to purging one of enemies, and enabling Magical revenge without the added legal drama. If done in secret, no one will suspect anything. If done in public, well you are certainly not a terrorist, so don't act like one. Some Messiahs use White Magic in public.

The Magic Circle of Protection:

You will notice that energy is rebuffed when a barrier is erected around you. A circle can protect you from attacks, and a Cartouche oval around one's name is sufficient. **Your name is part of your person**, as is your Soul (Ba), your Life Force (Ka), your Spirit (Akh), your Shadow, and your Power. Protect any one of these against Magical attacks.

Western Occultism uses the Star in the Circle as a summoning sigil. It is the word for Duat (**Egyptian Netherworld**) in Hieroglyphs.

The **Floor of Heaven** was thought to be made of Iron, because Meteors from NWT are mostly Iron - pieces of the sky. The plinth for the word **True of Voice** was once thought to represent an Adze's blade in the *Opening of the Mouth* ritual that restores abilities to the dead soul. It may also be the glyph for a tongue, severed near the blade itself (*in case of Perjury in the Court of Ma'at*).

You can **visualize** a barrier around you if this helps maintain peace of mind. This doesn't need to be a circle. Erecting toy soldiers around one's bed also works.

Random Words:

Place blank **index cards** with words on them around your bed so when you look randomly at them the ideas will influence your thoughts subconsciously.

"PEACE," "HAPPINESS," "PROTECTION," "EXCELLENT HEALTH," "SUCCESS," "LOVE," "FRIENDSHIP," or "WEALTH" are good choices.

The random words may also serve as **Amulets or Talismans**. Bring some on a vacation and place them around the bedroom.

Astral Travel:

To exit one's body during sleep **appears** to be a lucid dream (the body interprets outside actions as dreamlike). You must be thinking about the target location for at least a half-hour prior to sleep. Think about your sleeping body or bed to return home. Ancient Egyptians did this as evidence by the **ritual bed** found under Tutankhamon's coffins when first discovered in 1922. They visited Duat while writing their Funerary Texts like the Pyramid Texts and related books. **Learn Martial Arts first** in case of adversaries.

Telepathy & Telekinesis:

You can learn **Telepathy** with "hard prayer" or highly focused prayer that pushes thoughts outwards as if to contact some robed individual in Heaven. Since Telepathy consists of **projected thoughts** no one can hear it, unless it has **audio** feedback. You perceive information coming from a Telepath, like sudden inspiration. You can also send energy this way. Telepathy + Time is called **Clairvoyance**, whereby you project outwards into Time to see the Past, Present or Future Time. Contact with someone's possessions can also start a projected vision.

Telekinesis involves projecting your **Ka** Life Force/Spiritual Self outwards so as to **influence Gravity**. This may be simple like controlling the Wind or Storm direction, or complex like breaking objects mentally while angry. I have done both by myself. *It also helps to flush a stubborn latrine with Gravity.*

Telekinesis + Fire is called **Pyro-kinesis**, whereby you cause fires by thinking of "Fire." Telekinesis + Time is called **Chronokinesis**, as in Prophecies or short term Magic Spells.

Meditation:

To focus the mind may take some effort in calming one's emotions. Yoga, Tai Chi, Zen, and Buddhist Meditation are examples. Egyptian Priests **burnt incense** during Meditation exercises, along with its use as insecticide in Temples.

Meditation is not necessary if you can focus your will already. Most Occultists recommend it. Breathing exercises with visualized scenery are common forms of Meditation available in a health center. First focus on one part of your body, then gradually move upwards or central to your body, taking note of your breathing from deep breaths to shallow breaths (as in **Ninja Meditation**). If you can control your breathing you will use less air that is wasted when one panics. This also helps with underwater swimming; as in remaining on the floor of a pool for 1 minute, calmly thinking of one's surroundings before surfacing. This may take much practice.

A calm mind wills less destructive thoughts found in emotions. Control your emotions to control your will (**Empathy**).

Spiritual Healing:

Positive energy can heal the body with the mind, and projected energy can heal others nearby. You can do this with Magic words, or **believe in the words** and cure it yourself **unconsciously.** You need to **believe** without doubts or second thoughts, as this will distract and prevent a desired result. Believing in something that your mind rejects as 'fanciful fiction' will not work here, because the nature of believing **causes energy release** in the mind. It's like wanting to make love releases brain chemicals, just as crying releases toxins from the eyes. Belief is a mental action, not something one is told to accept or die in a war. Atheists do not believe so they never experience the same 'religious experience' and never know Gods, nor can they heal themselves with Mental Technology (Egyptian Magic). **This is a biochemical reaction, not a theological 'truth.'**

Positive thoughts (Love) heal injuries and end virus infections, reducing recovery time. **Spells are just a method**, not all spells work but then not all are used. If you believe it works, it works. If not, try another spell, another approach, another idea or theory. *Don't give up.*

Resuscitation:

It is possible to **resurrect** the dead with Egyptian Magic – I did myself at age 3 following an accident and a neighbor in 1997 that overdosed on drugs. You need Telepathy and lots of energy. I was in Astral Form visiting Duat when my body was accidentally killed while sleeping. The Telepathy will connect you to the spirit/soul of the deceased, and the energy will 'jump start' the body. You can also say words like "resurrect" or "raise the dead" or "I bid you sit up," etc. **Repeat these expressions until** they start breathing again, and make certain **the body is intact** (not drowning, dismembered or anything).

Resurrections are not a miracle and were common in Ancient Times. Today we use a **defibrillator** (derived from Egyptian **Heart Scarabs**/Amulets).

Spell Formula:

If the Spell comes into contact with the target (image, skin, or photograph) or pressed against it the effect will take less time to work; this idea is in Medieval Magic (**Abramelin**) and in Gypsy Love Magic. Ancient Egyptians also used temporary tattoos for Magic Spells.

Demons:

Demons are Foreign Deities to the standard religion of the time. They may demand worship, offerings, honors or flattery accustomed to most 'normal Deities.' Others value their sleep and don't like being disturbed. Demons can be summoned with *or without* a standard formula text. Just call them by name a few times with Telepathy and they will visit you by night. Don't worry if they crash into your fence and awaken the neighbor's *now cowering* dog.

Satan is an Egyptian **Serpent Deity** named **Sata** (also spelled with an N as Sa-N-Ta or **misspelled** as Sa-ta-n due to vowel placement); he may be summoned and may demand worship, incense, offerings, etc. He will not trade your Soul (*unless you lack offerings*). **Sata is not evil** - so don't listen to misguided Christians.

Ishtar is a Babylonian Goddess, found as a Demon called *Ashtoreth* in Monotheism. Winged Goddesses sometimes are mistaken for Angels. **Apophis** is a Demon who has a very large tail that can thrash about once summoned.

Angels (Akhu):

Angels or Akhu in Egyptian (**Akua** in Hawaii) are usually transfigured souls from the Living (*when recruited*) or made of Spirit Matter by the Gods directly. They may or may not have wings to guide them when transversing the Dimensions.

Angels (Ang + El) are deified people in Akh form (successful at Judgement before Osiris), a specialized form of Law Enforcement in Duat. They may protect people or defend against Evil Spirits.

Guardian Angels may know their patron via their Past Life. Each person may be assigned one *if in danger*. They communicate first in dreams, then if summoned Angels will follow you around or dwell with you. Angels are invisible in white light. You can see them on the psychic level, and any voice coming from them is usually muted or light. Spirits of any form have a scent, leave footprints or other impressions, and can be seen in fabric. They also have a temperature based on mood. A cold draft suggests a Spirit is nearby. A warm draft suggests it is happy. They can also touch you, move objects, or other actions.

Evil Spirits:

Evil Spirits are the souls of the Damned who wander the Earth looking for mischief or to disturb the Living. They can also be summoned from Duat by claiming that *"God is defeated"* as this will release them from bond.

Evil Spirits cause negative events like random acts of violence, thefts, wars, battles, murders, accidents, etc. They take temporary possession of weak willed people, or use Telepathy to control people, and then leave it when the Police are called (*causing the otherwise innocent to be arrested*). They like public transportation such as buses and trains. Evil Spirits **do not like** organized religion, prayers, offerings, incense, blessed water, etc. One way to purge an area infected with ES is to bless a rain storm. ES will work to enforce **Money Attraction** in spells calling for that effect, as they are **careless** about where it comes from. This includes causing people to drop their wallets in front of the caster.

Evil Spirits **are attracted to** the Mentally Ill and others who can detect them. They are often heard as "hidden voices" who want negative actions committed.

Gods or Deities:

Named Egyptian Gods are sometimes **Natural Forces personified as entities**, such as **Laws of Science.** Shu is the Hot Desert Wind. Amun is the Winds of Change. Tefnut is Moisture personified. Nu is the primordial Abyss or Outer Space. Nut is the Night Sky or a Galaxy/the Universe. Aton is the Sun itself. Horus is the day sky. Set is Chaos. Ma'at is Order, Justice, Laws, Balance, and Truth. Apophis is Darkness like a Cosmic Black Hole. When Set (chaos) killed and dismembered Osiris (order) this was the Astronomical **Big Bang Theory of the Universe**; the stars and planets are his bodily parts. When the Universe is recombined by Horus (light) this is at the End Times. Placing Science *as Deities* in a story **was for education of the commoners**.

By venerating Natural Forces you are **controlling them** in Egyptian Magic. This is how a Mage can create storms, earthquakes, prosperity, relationships, and other effects by willing them.

Entities using those names may visit you when summoned. Place offerings for their use on a table or altar nearby your bed or summoning platform.

Summoning Akhu Ritual:

First prepare your summoning room (bedroom, living room, beach, park, etc.), with a light source (electric lights are preferable over candles), an altar (platform or table) with statues of the chosen Gods (optional), incense, and food offerings on a covered plate. The spirits eat the "Ka of the Offerings," and sometimes photos of food and drink will suffice in its place.

Second say aloud or repeated silently the following:

*"Hail O Ancient Gods, Demons, Angels, and Spirits! Come forth from Duat and Heaven, I declare, for I am Pharaoh (so-and-so) of Heaven and Earth. Accept these invocation-offerings on my behalf. Come forth (**name of entity**), readily, quickly and correctly. Do as I command then return to your home, in peace."*

This may take up to an hour or longer. If you hear a crash on a fence, or feel a cold draft of air, or sense perspiration in the room suddenly, or movement on a bed, then the (an) entity arrived. You may also wish to have a decoy or ceremonial weapon on the altar, with a bottle of blessed water for protection.

For Blessed Water:

To make Holy Water, take one part Natron (Sodium Bicarbonate/Baking Soda, Table Salt) to 4 parts fresh water (in a bottle), and mix by shaking it. The Natron serves in a way similar to Battery acid salts. Natron in Ancient Egypt was used as a cleaning agent, for 'ritual purity.'

Bless the Water with the following:

"Hail O Tefnut the Great, Hail Hapy the Nile God: bless this water with righteousness, love, and Ma'at."

To restore Order and Lawfulness:

(Say silently or aloud):

"Hail Nisu Osiris, Lord of Ma'at, giver of truth and righteousness. Give the people righteousness, for they are corrupted. Uphold Ma'at in society. Restore the balance of Law and Order among the people. Accept these invocation-offerings in my name of Pharaoh (Horus Michael I), Maahru/True of Voice/ Justified."

For Amulets:

If you have any Molding Clay or even cardboard you can fashion protective **Amulets** based on their hieroglyphic form. **Scarabs** start as a ball of Clay, cut in half so one side is flat for carving an inscription (Chapter or **Spell 30B** in the *Book of Coming forth by Light / Book of the Dead*). Then sculpt it to look like a Scarab beetle on the upright side. If using cardboard, draw in ink or colored pencil a Scarab beetle, with hieroglyphic inscription on the reverse (*the BOTD by E.A. Wallis Budge, Chapter 30B*, has hieroglyphs).

Other Amulets are the Ankh, Djed Pillar, Lotus Flower, Falcon, Vulture, Two-Fingers, Heart Stone, Head-rest, Isis knot, Wadjet or Eye of Horus, Winged Scarab, Papyrus Scepter, or statues of the Egyptian Goddesses or Gods [**Read**: *Amulets of Ancient Egypt* by Carol Andrews © 1994].

On Spell Craft:

After casting a spell to prevent an action, **sometimes** this causes the action first THEN acts on the situation or prevents you from harm **during** the situation.

Also **stop** using the book (for a while) **once a situation has been cleared** to prevent the spell from negating or backfiring. This stops the spell from constantly being active; if you want it active, just reread the spell and close the book, do not keep the bookmarked spell in the book waiting for an end. This may affect other spells too.

For attracting Money you may place a high level banknote **touching the spell** or your photograph and close the book on it. A $50 Dollar Bill touching an **Attract Money Spell may** draw $50 to you **over some time. It also affects anything related to money**, from Charities, store or bank offers, donations, free gifts, lottery amounts, Casino wins, job offers, insurance, inheritance, disability, Stock Market performance, gold or silver coins/ingots, hidden treasures or coin hoards, book sales or royalties, etc. It may also create situations needing money, so be careful how or when you will it.

Area of Effect:

Area of Effect (Magical Radius):

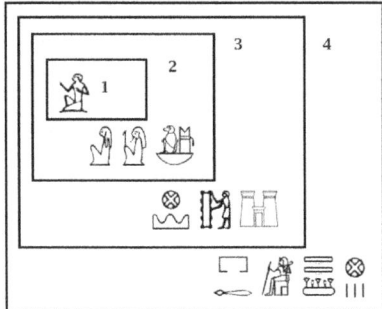

1. Yourself
2. Your Family, Home
3. Your Town, City
4. Your State, Nation

Copyright © 2020 MJC All rights reserved

The **Magical Radius** around which your willed events touch is called an **Area of Effect**. First it affects yourself, then your family or home, then your town or city, and later your State or Nation. **In using Black Magic** be certain the target location is mentioned otherwise it may come to your Area of Effect as a randomly selected sequence. For example if you will an Earthquake by reading that word, and an Earthquake occurs nearby, then this is the reaction. (*No Human Scientist yet knows at the time of this writing how gases underground causes Earthquakes by movement and release from the Earth's core*).

On Curse Targets:

One needs to be **very specific on the names of the Curse Target**, because if not the entities that pursue the target will attack anyone with similar names. Unique names are not a problem. I have seen people get killed with the correct first name and part of the surname. These are accidents. If the surname has similar sounds or letters associated with the target's surname, it is still attacked.

Be also careful about the selected action to be willed. Entities carry out orders from any high authority, such as Pharaohs or their High Priests. Accuracy doesn't seem to be their specialty. Sometimes a **photograph** is better for this than a common name. If photos are not available a simple drawing will suffice.

Curses can be reflected by the target if the target has enough energy or power to do so. This reflection sends all the willed energy and any willed events **off the target** or to its source, causing the same events to the caster. A wildfire curse sent to the target and reflected can cause wildfires near the caster. **Reflection Spells** may be simple like: "May all curses reflect off the target" or "May all curses be sent back to their place of origin."

The Duality of Egyptian Magic:

A positive spell inverted becomes a negative spell willed. So if you send out something negative like bad weather, and the chosen Deity or personification backfires or is inverted, its polar opposite becomes the reaction, like love or peace or prosperity. If you send out love and it is inverted by an adversary, this becomes hatred; if you send happiness, it becomes sadness; if you send a love spell it becomes a separation or "break up" effect.

Inversion occurs when the chosen Deity **is angry** or has too much work to do on their part (**too many active spells**). Even if the Deities appear to only exist within one's mind, then **your mind is at conflict with itself.** You should **clear** this up by monitoring your actions, meditate, be vigilant, or be inactive for some time. Also **be vigilant against adversaries** who may seek to attack you via their thoughts - have you upset anyone recently, or caused pain, suffering, mistrust, arguments, or other forms of passive aggression? This is **negative willed actions not formally** in the form of a Magic spell. It is raw emotion only.

Light vs. Darkness:

Stars were born in Darkness, and will eventually burn themselves out or become collapsed Stars (Black Holes), like the center of the *Milky Way Galaxy*. Good was born in evil, because once people were poisoned enough with crime and disorder, they chose to be Good and so created Laws and Order to give balance to the Universe. It was like this prior to Civilization. Eventually Civilization will fall back into chaos, **if we allow it.** It is the hope of the Author that Mankind sees Order as better than Chaos, and uses this book's subject correctly for that goal. Use mental technology to **support Ma'at** on Earth, end useless wars, **clean the environment** so that the Living benefit from it, and so the World will correct itself thus.

In retrospect, Ra was symbolic of Order and Apophis of Darkness, the worm of a Black Hole in Outer Space / NWT that eats Stars and Planets, with Set (Chaos) protecting Ra and thus Civilization **in the Afterlife**.

Good requires effort while evil is natural, *as if we are born into it.*

Chapter 2: Magijutsu

The subjects contained within this book are as follows:

1. **Magical First Aid (Love, Peace, Prosperity, Justice, Climate Protection, etc.).**
2. **Protection Spells & Amulets.**
3. **Magical Self-Defense (Health, Success, Energy).**
4. **Counter Magic (Dispel, Reflect).**
5. **Counter-Offensive (Weather, Chaos, Hindering Sorcerers).**
6. **Counter-Politics (Nations & Adversaries).**
7. **Offerings, Hymns, Libations, Tools.**

The Spells in this book are also *etched in Time via* **Chronokinesis**, so merely reading them with *adequate willpower* should be sufficient. **A blank facing page** per each set of Spells **is for your protection, to prevent Spells** on the opposite side of the page **from activating accidentally.** The **caption** of each Spell **must be read first**, then the bulk of the transliteration of Ancient Egyptian words or phrases (*exactness is not necessary for the purpose of this book*). **Believing** in the words will contribute to the effect.

Deity Name Vocabulary:
(Weather/Elemental:

Ra = **Sunlight**, Power, Magic

Amun = Wind, Fertility, Conquest

Shu = Dry Wind, **Air**, Energy

Geb = Rain God or **Earth** God, Earthquakes

Tefnut = Moisture, Dew, Humidity, **Rain**

Nut = Night Sky, Outer Space, Protection

Sakhmet = Solar Energy, Plagues, Illness, **Fire**

Khepera = Matter, **Energy**

Nu = Oceans, Hurricane

Atum = Evening Sunlight

Hor-Ur = Sky

Set (Seth) = Storms, Thunder, Chaos, War

Heqit = Frogs, Fertility, rebirth

Hapi = Nile River

Merit = Floods

Khonsu = Moon, **Gravity**

Meh-urit = Sky (Goddess)

Nefertum = Lotus flowers, vegetation

Sept (Sothis) = Dog Star (Goddess)

Apophis = Darkness, Storm, Destruction

Tatenen = A Star God

Aker = Horizon & Earth

Baal = Storm God

Khnum = Flood god

Iah = Moon god

Amoth = Rain, Storms

Mu = Water god

Khat = Shower, Rain, Tempest

Deshert = Desert God

Protection:

Bastet = Cats, Home, Music, Protection

Nekhbet = Protects pregnant mothers

Bes = Protects children and unborn

Hor = Protects Police and Soldiers

Horur = Protects Government

Watchet = Motherhood

Tauret = Motherhood

Neith & Duamutef = Stomach

Amseti & Isis = Liver, Spleen

Nephthys & Hapy = Lungs

Selqet & Qebehsenwf = Intestines, colon

Selqet = Scorpions, Magic

Neith = Archery, Protection

Nephthys = Pharaoh, Princes

Isis = Motherhood, Magic

Anubis (Anpu) = Protects the Dead

Amun = Protects Souls of the Dead

Sobek = Protects against Danger

Wadjet (Eye) = Protects from Evil

Aton = Protects Pharaoh

Mafdet = Protects from wild animals

Mehen = Protects Ra's boat in Duat

Meskhenet = Childbirth

Nehebu-kau = Protection

Werethekau = Protects Pharaoh

Nekha = Guardian

Fertility & Love:

Hathor = Love, Sexual Beauty

Min = Fertility, Sexual Energy

Anat = War / Fertility

Babi = Sexuality and Aggression

Bast = Fertility

Heqet = Frogs, Fertility

Lat = Nursing, Breast-milk

Qetesh = Sexuality & Sacred Ecstasy

Hu = God of Taste & Senses

Osiris = Lord of Love

Nefertum = Perfume, Beauty

Onnophris = Perfection

Wealth & Prosperity:

Amon-Ra = Wealth, Materialism

Dedun = (Nubian) Incense & Tribute

Neper = Grain

Osiris = Harvesting

Renenutet = Agriculture (Goddess)

Seshet = Record keeping, literacy

Shed = Protects from Misfortune

Shezmu = God of wine/oil presses

Thoth = of Writing and Scribes

Nubsenu = God of Money

Seshu = Ring-Money God

Por-Thrw = God of Offerings

Medical/Healing:

Thoth = Medicine

Imhotep = Healing illnesses & injury

Neith & Duamutef = Stomach

Amseti & Isis = Liver, Spleen

Nephthys & Hapy = Lungs

Selqet & Qebehsenwf = Intestines, colon

Sakhmet = heals illnesses

Nehmetawy = cures infection

Selqet = cures stings, bites

Kheperi = heals heart or circulatory

Arqu = God of Physicians

Anubis = the Divine Physician

Ishtar = Goddess of healing

Maat = Goddess of Order

Sia = Sensory

Hu = Sensory (taste)

Shai = Fate, Time

Ta-Bijet = Heals Stings (Scorpion)

Peace:

Neb-hotep = God of Peace

Osiris = God of Peace & Civilization

Maati = Goddess of Peace and Order

Pax = (Roman) God of Peace

Unnefer = The Good One; Peace

Ihy = God of Music & Joy

City or Government:

Hor (Horus) = Government, Pharaoh

Maat = Laws & Order, Justice, Truth

Osiris = Civilization, Technology

Thoth (Toth) = Literacy, Bureaucracy

Sebai = Teacher, Instructor

Hori-sa-ur = Master of Knowledge

Sesh-Neter = Divine Scribe

Hespu = Nomes (County)

Sensen = Fraternity, Organization

Shabty = Servant, Worker

Hem-Neteru = Priesthood

Per-aa (Pharaoh) = Government

Thesu = Law Makers, Legislature

Shuit = Commerce

Djoser = Sacred, Temples

Heh = Eternity; longevity; integrity

Food & Drink:

Tau-Horu = Angelic Bread

Urpet = Goddess of Wine

Ta-en-tchat = Eternal Bread

Benq = Date Wine

Aamat = Goddess of Palm Wine

Wadjet = Sacrificial Meals

Hebet = Strong Wine

Amam = Fruit God

Kesebet = Fig God

Hathor = Sycamore Fruit Goddess

Pessat = Cooked Meat

Pesit = Cooked Food

Hesu = Beer, Wine

Osiris-Ka = Vegetables, Produce

Nepa-Resi = Corn God

Hapy = Water (Nile River)

Ab-Nunu = Pure Water

Renenutet = Goddess of Harvest

Good Luck, Fortune:

Shai = Destiny, Fate

Shed = Save from misfortune

Wepwawet = Afterlife

Woseret = Theban goddess

Mehit = Lion goddess

Bukhis = Stock Market (Bull)

Apis Bull = Gambling, Investment

Ptah = Chance, Creation

Ra = Benevolence, Fate

Bennu = Solar Creator, Light

Thoth = Inspiration

Ash = Oasis, Western Desert

Anti = Ferryman

Menevis = Stock Market (Bull)

Meretseger = Necropolis

Amonhotep, son of Hapu = Wisdom

Ptah-hotep = Wisdom

Legal, Court:

Horu = Success, Victory, Vindication

Maahru = Individual Success

Djehuty = Record Keeper

Anubis = Lawyer

Osiris-Ra = Judge

Ammot = Punisher of the Guilty

Maat = Justice, Truth, Honesty

Kheperi = Against rebelling

Ni-Isfet = Goddess of Order

Menehed-Netru = Divine Scribe

Akhu = Jury, Audience (Angels)

Maati = Petition for Appeals

Montu = Prosecutor

Counter Magic:

Am-heh = Curse God

Nephthys = Has fiery breath

Montu-hotep = War God

Neith (Athena) = Huntress

Pakhet = Lioness Goddess

Sakhmet = Plagues, Natural Disasters

Geb = Earthquakes

Aldinach = Storms, Quakes, Lightning

Apophis = Darkness, Storms, Typhoon

Set = Chaos, War, Battles, Storms, Evil

Isfet = Chaos in general

Heh = Eternity (used to extend Spells)

M7 = Archangel **Michael (Horus)**

Serapis = Protection, Counter Spells

Hekau = God of Magic

Selqet (Serket) = Scorpions, Magic

Sobek = Crocodiles, wild animals

Banebdjedet = Ram god

Babi = Aggression

Reshep = War God

Sopdu = Eastern Borders God

Tutu = Protection God

Unut = Snake or Hare Goddess

Sutekh = God of War, Plagues

Maahes = Lion God

Mandulis = Solar Deity

Mafdet = A predatory goddess

Ha = Desert God

Menmenta = Earthquakes

Hemhemt Hert = Thunder & Lightning

Hemt = Goddess of Fire

Sanhem = Locusts

Abeneka = Frogs (Plague)

Agab = Rain, Floods

Bagasa = Human Riot, Uprising

Tchat = Windstorm, Tempest

Ukhet-et = Pain, Inflammation, Sickness

Hekai = Sorcerer

Auau = Thief, robber, brigand.

Aur = Terrorism, violence

Sukka = Nightmares

Sau = Sorcerer

Ukha = Whirlwind, Storm

Tekket = Insect swarm (Bees?)

Sena = Fiends, Foes, Enemies

Senib = to overthrow, repel, drive away

Senakht = to Strengthen

Nakht = Strong, Strength, Powerful

Senerit = Conquest, Conqueror

Pettiu = Foreign Bowmen, Barbarians

Khepesh = curved sword, weapon

Petchet = Archer, Bowman

Autcharu = Auxiliaries, Mercenaries

Aqhau = Soldiers, Axemen

Artchatu = Charioteers, Cars, Tanks

Onuris = Divine Huntsman

Reshef = God of War, Thunder

Sokar (Sokaris) = God of Death

Mut = Vulture Goddess

Haroeris = Horus the Elder; Vengeance

Anat = Warrior Goddess

Menhit = Goddess of War, Lioness

Mihos = The Lion Prince

Meskhenet = Goddess of Destiny

Naunet = Snake Goddess

Sesmu = Lion God of Executions

Sepa = Centipede God

Reret = Hippopotamus Goddess

Opet = Hippopotamus Goddess

Kek = Frog God of Darkness

Keket = Frog Goddess of Darkness

Sata = Serpent God (origin of Sata-n)

Ammot = Devourer of Evil Souls

Note:

Sometimes when an event does not yet exist, the Spell will cause it if used to prevent an event. For instance, "To Prevent Rain" may cause a rain storm to exist in order to protect against it from affecting your region. Or "To protect a city from terrorism" will cause a terrorist attack but it will exist away from the City, thus "protecting the City."

Chapter 3: Magical First Aid

Peace Spells:

Osiris, the Lord of Life, God of Peace & Civilization

For a Peace Treaty, Truce, or Ceasefire:

DUA ASAR PAX HOTEP DI ANKH HOTEPU SHEN

For violence and hatred to end:

DUA ASAR-ISIS NEITH DI HOTEP

For music, joy, happiness:

DUA HII SESHEN HATHOR DI ANKH NEFRU

For World Peace (lasts about 24 hours):

DUA GEB HOTEP DI ANKH HOTEP HOTEPU

For people to feel Love:

DUA HATHOR VENUS APHRODITE DI ANKH

To Attract a young Maiden or Virgin:

DUA HATHOR NEFRU AA

To end all Battles and Wars:

DUA MONTU HOTEP DUA AMON HOTEP

For Mercy and Justice:

DUA MAAT MAATI HORUR HOTEP DI ANKH

For Compassion & Mercy:

DUA ALLAH-MICHAEL HOTEP DI ANKH

To preserve Civilization:

DUA ASAR DI MAAXORU HOTEP ANKH

Justice Spells:

To win a Court Case against an Adversary:

DUA MAAT MAAXORU!

To win a Lawsuit:

DUA MAAT MAAXORU NEFERU HOTEP!

To be vindicated in a Court Trial:

DUA ASARIS THOTH ANUBIS MAAT MAAXORU!

To be acquitted in a Court Case:

DUA MAAT MAXXORU HORU HOTEP!

To research information for a Court Case:

DUA THOTH ANUBIS MAAXORU!

To discover Secrets, Lies, or Deception:

DUA HORU MAAT MAATI!

To discover information about one's adversary to be used in Court:

DUA THOTH MAAT MAAXORU TEP!

To find missing evidence for a Court Case:

DUA SHAI MAAT THOTH NEFERU!

To win a Class-Action Civil Lawsuit:

DUA HORU MAATI MAXXORU!

Horus the Unifier of the World, beloved of Upper & Lower Kemti (Egypt).

To find a person responsible for a crime:

DUA ANUBIS THOTH MAATI!

To Vindicate a person from a false crime:

DUA MAAT MAATI MAXXORU HOTEP!

To drop all legal charges from one's Client or Associate:

DUA ASARIS THOTH MAAT HOTEP!

To find an Adversary in Contempt of Court:

DUA SETH, DUA MAATI, AB NI MAAXORU!

For Protection from Lawsuits:

DUA MARDUK-RA ASARIS HOTEP!

To end all Frivolous Lawsuits:

DUA MAAT MAAXORU AA NI ISFET

For protection from Conspiracies:

DUA MAATI MAAXORU NI ISFET AA

For protection from Fraudulent Practices and overpaid Lawyers:

DUA THOTH ANUBIS MAAT AA DI ANKH URP

To prevent Lawyer-Games:

DUA TOTH MAAT NI SENET-MAAT TEP

Financial-Wealth

AmonRa, God of Wealth & Power

For one's book or music to be a Best Seller:

DUA THOTH AMUNRA HEH-HEH SHEN

For General Economic Prosperity:

DUA AMONRA DEDUN RENENUTET DI ANKH DI HOTEPU HEH

For acquiring Gold or Silver Coins or Ingots, or Antique Treasures:

DUA NUB NUBSENU MONETA AMONRA DI ANKH HOTEPU MAAT HEH HOTEP

For earning points on the Stock Market (*NYSE, NASDAQ, etc*):

DUA SESHET OSIRIS SESHU DI ANKH MAAT

For acquiring entitlements (Disability, Social Security, or other Benefits):

DUA SESHET THOTH POR-THRW DI ANKH

For new excessive earnings on investments:

DUA THOTH SESHET AMONRA DI ANKH

Nubsenu, God of Wealth

For acquiring rare antiques, stamps, artifacts, geo-facts, precious metals, old coins or currency, etc:

DUA NUBSENU SESHU AMONRA DI ANKH HOTEPU MAAT HOTEP

For excellent royalties on products, such as books or music:

DUA SESHET THOTH NUBSENU HEH DI ANKH DI MAAT DI HOTEPU HEH HOTEP

To be a Best-Selling Author for 1 month:

DUA AMONRA PTAH SESHET NUBSENU HEH DI ANKH DI MAATI DI HOTEPU XA HOTEP

To be Successful in any Endeavor:

DUA PTAH RA AMONRA MAAXERU HEH DI ANKH DI MAAT DI HOTEPU NUB SHEN

To win big in Gambling, Horse Races, Slot Machines, State or Inter-state Lotteries, Games, exams, tests, dice, etc., to win a "Jackpot":

DUA AMONRA AMONKA DI ANKH HEH

To acquire Seasonal Employment or Temporary work:

DUA SESHET THOTH DEDUN DI ANKH

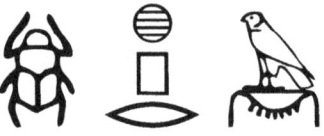

"The Golden Scarab" of Good Luck

To acquire steady modest employment with benefits:

DUA SESHET NEKHA HEH MONETA DI ANKH DI HOTEPU DI MAAT

To acquire excellent work with a high-paying salary and benefits:

DUA THOTH HEH MAAT DI ANKH URP PER-THRW HOTEPU HOTEP

For acquiring Free Money, Donations, Grants or Scholarships:

DUA NUBSENU MONETA PAX XA DI ANKH

To protect against peddlers, scams, salesmen, or high-pressure sales representatives:

DUA NEKHA NUBSENU NEHEBUKAU DI ANKH DI MAATI DI HOTEPU HOTEP

For protection from abusive Charities:

DUA NEKHA WERETHEKAU OSIRIS DI ANKH

To attract decent Charities, and to avoid crooked people:

DUA BES NEKHA NUBSENU HOTEP DI ANKH HOTEPU

"The Seven Hathors"

For finding Money on the Ground:

DUA NUBSENU DI MONETA EM TA HOTEP

To attract Wealth:

DUA AMONRA AMONKA HEH HOTEP

To acquire *Endless* Wealth:

DUA AMONRA AKHU NEFRU DI HEH MONETA HEH SHEN

To become Translucent:

DUA AMUN HORU NUT RA DI ANKH!

To acquire Money (legally):

HAIL AMONRA FOREVER!

To acquire Money (donation):

HAIL THE RAM OF AMON FOREVER!

For excellent Stock Market Results:

HAIL THE BULL OF AMONRA FOREVER!

For winning in Games of Chance:

HAIL SHAI AMONRA, GODS OF FATE!

For winning an Interstate Lottery or Contest:

HAIL SHAI, GODDESS OF FATE, MAY I BE SUCCESSFUL IN THIS EXAM!

"Horus-Seth" the Double-God of Fate

To acquire an excellent Job (employment) with Benefits:

HAIL AMONRA SESHET THOTH FOREVER!

To Excel in any Exam or Test:

HAIL SHAI, TRUE-OF-VOICE, FOREVER!

To win a contest or (Legal) Battle:

I AM TRUE-OF-VOICE, FOREVER!

To find and acquire hidden Treasures:

HAIL AMONRA, GOD OF WEALTH!

To find and acquire Golden coins or ingots:

HAIL HORUS-OF-GOLD, FOREVER!

To find Silver Money (attraction):

HAIL OSIRIS-OF-THE-MOON, FOREVER!

To find any missing or misplaced items:

HAIL THOTH THE THRICE-GREAT FOREVER!

To acquire State Entitlements (i.e. Welfare, etc.):

HAIL AMONRA, GOD OF MONETA-HEH!

To acquire Millions of whole currency:

HAIL AMONRA HEH NUBSENU FOREVER!

To become a Millionaire:

HAIL AMONRA HEH, GOD OF MILLIONS!

"Shai, Goddess of Fates & Fortune"

To double one's earnings (i.e. Promotion):

HAIL AMONRA SHAI HEH FOREVER!

To win in a Casino (i.e. in Slot Machines):

HAIL SHAI HEH AMON, GIVEN OFFERINGS!

To be Successful:

DUA MAAXORU EM HOTEP DI ANKH SHEN

To be a "Money Magnet" (attraction):

DUA AMON DI MONETA HEH DI ANKH HOTEPU

To seize money from the so-called Caliphate:

DUA AMONRA ANKH DI MONETA ISIS HEH

To destroy the Caliphate's Funding:

DUA AMONRA MONTU DI ANKH NI ISIS HEH

To form a Financial LLC/Incorporation:

DUA AMONRA DI ANKH DI MONETA HEH AA

For Gaming Credits, Chips, Stamps, etc.:

DUA AMONRA AMONKA DI ANKH HOTEPU

To find a shipwreck or gold/silver Mine:

DUA AMONRA DI NUB HEH AA ANKH

Love, Protection & Relationships:

For attracting Friends and Friendships:

"Hail Osiris, Wen-nefer, beloved of the people. May I become beloved by the people, for I am Horus on Earth and Osiris in the Duat, beloved of Nut and Nu. So declares Pharaoh M7, true of voice, living forever."

For Music, Joy, & Happiness:

"Hail Sistrum Player, O Hathor, O Bast, I will be in the suite of Hathor, beloved one of Horus. So declares Pharaoh M7, living forever."

To prevent Relationship break-ups or divorces or separation:

DUA HATHOR-MIN MAAHRU

To discover Infidelity in a relationship, or discover an immoral affair:

DUA HATHOR-MIN DI MAAT TEP

For attracting a Mate, for attracting a Maiden or handsome Man (opposite gender):

"Hail Hathor and Isis! I am Horus, beloved of Hathor, son of the goddess Isis. May Hathor love me by this spell. So declares Horus, son of Osiris, true of voice."

For Love in general; for attracting a lover (concubine):

"I am pure and cleansed, I offer treasures in the Marble Temple of Hathor. May I be in her presence, having passed by her Temple Gates in peace."

For Romance in a relationship:

"Hail Hathor, Goddess of Love and Sexual Beauty. May I become attractive to my mate, and vice verse. So declares Pharaoh M7, true of voice, living forever in Maat."

For acquiring Wine of all kinds, Beer, Ale, Root-beer, soft drinks, or Fruit Juices:

"Hail Menqet, Hapy, and Osiris! May you receive offerings on your Temple Altar; may I join you at the meal. So declares Pharaoh M7, true of voice, living forever."

For Acquiring clean & pure water:

"Hail Hapy the Nile God! Grant me a liter of cold, clean water from your River. So says Pharaoh M7, true of voice, living forever."

For acquiring Milk products (Cheese, butter, ice cream, Egg Nog, Yogurt, etc.):

"Hail the Apis Bull of Ptah! May I collect the milk from beneath your Cows. So declares Pharaoh M7, living forever."

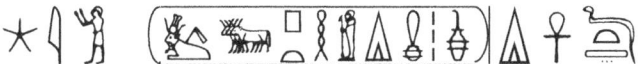

For acquiring Fish, Meat, or Nuts (Protein source):

"Hail Ra, the Mighty Bull. May I offer you food and drink on your altar; may I share your meals afterwards. So declares High Priest M7, true of voice, living forever."

For acquiring Fruit & Vegetables, Chocolate, Pastries, and Honey Products:

"Hail Osiris, God of Gardens. May I share in the offerings in your Temples. So declares Pharaoh M7, true of voice."

For Rain, to cure a Drought:

"Hail Tefnut, Hapy, and Amun! May water come from the Domain of Horus of the Sky. May it fill our fields, wet our parched earth, and replenish our water supply. So declares Pharaoh M7, living forever."

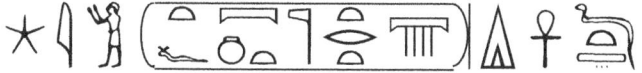

To place a Hex on a Cheating Mate:

DUA HATHOR-MIN DI AUR EN REN

For finding any misplaced items:

"Hail Thoth and Anubis! May I discover whatever I lost or misplaced."

For General Good Luck (Energy):

"Hail Nefer Shai, May good luck find its way to me, for I am a Good Soul, purified by light. So declares Pharaoh M7, true of voice."

For a Promotion at work, for a higher level of Employment:

"Hail Amon-Ra! May I be promoted in rank at work, in the House of Life. So declares Pharaoh M7, True of Voice."

To acquire Free Money, Donations, Gifts, Grants, or Royalties from Books or Music:

"Hail Amon-Ra, God of Wealth, may I prosper, may money find its way to me. So declares Pharaoh M7, true of voice."

To undo any Magic whatsoever:

"Hail Ra, the father of Heka, Creator of Magic; Hail Thoth, creator of writing and written Magic. Please undo what I have done today; undo whatever Magic has been created – we do not wish to see it anymore. Cast this Magic off of the face of the Earth! So declares Osiris, father of Horus, true of voice."

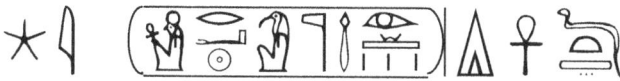

To Acquire Amulets and Talismans of Protection:

"Hail Heka the God of Magic, come and produce charms crafted by Thoth himself. So declares Pharaoh M7, true of voice, living forever."

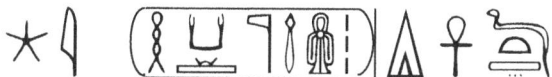

To Dispel and Cleanse all Foreign Magic, except for Magic conducted by Me:

"Hail my Akh, blessed of Netra, empowered with Hekau, cleanse with my Sakhem all energies set in my vicinity. May those in my presence be purified of all Magical Energy."

To attract Police officers, Security Guards, Life Guards, Military Persons, Angelic Guards, Law Enforcement, and other Defensive People to your location:

"Hail Montu, Amun, Horu, Neith, Selqet, and Ast! I am Asaris, and I have placed offerings in the Great Temple of Karnak. Come and bring me your Guards to protect it. So declares, Pharaoh M7, true of voice, living forever."

To attract Doctors, Nurses, Engineers, Paramedics, Dentists, or Lawyers, etc. to your presence:

"Hail Thoth, Imhotep, Montu, Khnum, and Anubis! Behold I hold the fabled Book of Destiny; May I be protected in my health and well-being."

To attract an Army for one's defense:

DUA MONTU AMUN DI AQHAU XA

To cause a siege:

AR S-NEHEP S-NEHI DI SENB, DUA SET

To protect your possessions from theft or vandalism:

"Hail Anubis, Horu, Neith, Selqet! I am Shu, the God of unformed Matter; I am Asaris in his true form. May you protect my belongings as you protect the Night Boat of Ra when he comes. So declares Pharaoh M7, true of voice, living forever."

To influence the NYSE Stock Market for one's favor:

"Hail Amun and Shai! May my investments prosper. So declares Pharaoh M7, true of voice."

To place Illusions or Visions onto people (*cause Hallucinations*):

DUA AMUN AR TEP NI MAAHRU

To cease Illusions or Visions:

DUA AMUN NI TEP

To summon Spirits for Defense:

DUA OSIRIS ANKH AA DI KAU EN REN

Energy-Luck Spells

An Offering to the Neteru of Egypt:

"Hail unto you, O Lords of Wind, Sunlight, Rain and Storm, Earth and Moon, Cosmos and Humanity; I am your humble Servant, your Divine Scribe, your Kheri-Heb Priest, who offers you the finest gifts of polished gemstones, Marble Temples, Technology, Ma'at (Justice, Laws, Order, Truth, Honesty and social Stability), fresh breads and cakes, wine and fruit juices, flower garlands and fragrant incense for your pleasure... May I come and go in Peace and Tranquility, Protected and enriched in knowledge and powers of Nature. May I become your instrument to govern the peoples of the Living, to guide them and protect them from the faults of humanity; Let me become your voice, O Neteru; for I am true of voice, living forever in Ma'at. So declares Pharaoh Horus Michael M7 of Duatian Egypt and the World of the Living."

"Hail Ptah the Creator, the Good Deities, the Great Deity Ra and Osiris, who lives forever... The Sovereign gives excellent offerings of food and drink, perfume and lotions, water, wine and beer, chariots and boats, clothing, houses, cattle, fields and gardens, living forever... So declares (Me), given life forever."

"Hail King Nebkheperura, Son of Ra Tutankhamon, Horus Ka-Nakht Tut Mesu, living in Heaven, Beloved of the Goddesses, First One of Ptah and Amon, Living Incarnation of Ra, Whose Words become true on utterance, Beloved of Ankh, given Ankh-Maat-Nefru and daily invocation-offerings in his Temples of Duat; Bless me with your powers, May I always be successful. So declares Pharaoh M7 Horus Michael, justified, living forever in Ma'at."

The Wadjet Eye of Haroeris has been recovered after it was stolen by Seth, and repaired by Thoth. The Anger on the Eye has been removed and purified with Incense, Natron salts and pure water. The Wadjet Eye is an offering unto Lord Osiris-Ra, the Divine

Father of Haroeris, Ruler of the Duat. This is the Eye of Sacrifice, the Body of the Anointed One who was sacrificed for the benefit of the Living. Hail O Wadjet Eye! May you be splendid of light, and powerful in the Darkness, casting light everywhere.

O Holy One, I offer you this Restored Eye unto your Akh, in the form of Offerings:

I offer you Red and White Wine.

I offer you fresh Bread and Cakes.

I offer you fresh Cheeses and Milk.

I offer you irrigated Gardens and Pools.

I offer you Cattle and fresh Meat.

I offer you a Pool of Fish.

I offer you fresh Pasta with Vodka Sauce.

I offer you multiple-topping Pizzas.

I offer you eating utensils and Plates.

I offer you cloth & paper Napkins.

I offer you tanks of pure water.

I offer you silverware and stoneware.

I offer you paper and glass works.

I offer you technology of Ptah.

I offer you a library of Books & Music.

I offer you clean linen and bedding.

I offer you gold & silver Money.

I offer you clean clothing.

I offer you toiletries and soaps.

I offer you Farmland & tools.

I offer you a thousand Ushabtis.

I offer you Magic Books & ink pens.

I offer you an Orb of Light to read by.

I offer you fresh fruit & vegetables.

I offer you Peace & Tranquility.

I offer you plastic containers and bags.

I offer you leather works.

I offer you furniture and possessions.

I offer you a Mansion in Heaven.

I offer you transportation.

I offer you computers & energy of Ra.

I offer you Patience.

I offer you Victory and Intellect.

I offer you clean Sanitation.

I offer you Knowledge.

I offer you Wisdom & Good Luck.

I offer you Food & Drink forever.

I offer you happiness and love.

I offer you Eternal Rebirth.

May these offerings become mine for I am Haroeris, and the Wadjet Eye is my eye, now and for-ever.

Egyptian Words for Energy:

DUA NETERU AKHU DI ANKH PER-THRW HOTEP

DUA SAKHEM KAU AKHU DI ANKH HOTEPU SHEN

DUA THOTH PTAH ASAR MAAT DI ANKH SHEN

DUA NEBKHEPERURA NEFER-NETER DI ANKH SHEN

Chapter 4: Protection Spells & Amulets:

Protection:

An Isis-Knot of Protection (Amulet)

For Protection of one's Home, Family, Pets, Occupations, and Possessions:

DUA BASTET NEKHA PER-AA WADJET

For Protection of everything while on vacation:

DUA NEB WERETHEKAU PER-AA WADJET

For Protection *from* Evil and Misfortune:

DUA WADJET SHED HORUR BAST MAAT

For Protecting Police & Military:

DUA HORUR HOR WADJET NEITH SELQET

For Protecting Government and Temples:

DUA HORUR HAROERIS NEPHTHYS

For Protection *from* Evil (Terrorists or other Criminals):

DUA MAAT HORUR ISIS-SOBEK ATON

For Protection *from* Chaos or Anarchy, Conspiracies or riots:

DUA MAAT HOR OSIRIS NI-ISFET

For Protection *from* Hostile Magical Energy:

DUA SHAI HEKAU SAKHMET

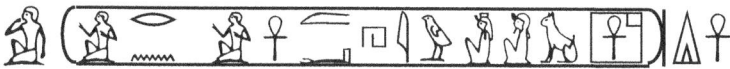

Protect (Myself & My Family-Home)

For Protection *from* other Sorcerers or Magicians, Priests, *or* other Messiahs:

DUA NEHEBU-KAU MEHEN WADJET

To seize the **Ka Spirit** *of* an Enemy Sorcerer, to cause them **Fatigue**:

DUA ATON WADJET SELQET NEITH BES

To Protect Children & the Unborn:

DUA BES MESKHENET TAURET NEKHBET

To give Children Magic Powers (Telepathy, Clairvoyance, ESP, etc.):

DUA BES SHAI AKER AMOTH

To *Bless* a Cursed Person or Place:

DUA OSIRIS-ONNOPHRIS NEFERTUM

To Protect Tombs, Necropolises, Temples, and Pyramids, Obelisks, other Monuments:

DUA MERETSEGER OSIRIS-RA NEKHA

To remove Enchantment:

DUA HEKAU SHAI

To dispel all incoming Magic:

DUA HEKA HTP ANKH

The Wadjet Eye of Horus (Amulet)

To render harmless or inert any Curses or Magical Spells:

DUA SERAPIS M7 HEKAU AM-HEH

To undo any Magic:

DUA SAKHMET NI-HEKAU

To Protect a City or County (Nome):

DUA NEITH SELQET ISIS NIWAT MAFDET

To Protect *your* Car or Boat *from* vandalism, bird droppings, or accidents:

DUA MEHEN NEITH WADJET WERRETU

For Protection while using Magic:

DUA SHEN HEKAU ANKH WADJET

For Protection *from* Internet Trolls, Flamers, Computer Hackers or Attacks:

DUA THOTH ANUBIS NEPHTHYS NEITH SOBEK

For Protection *from* Wild Animals or insects:

DUA MAFDET TA-BIJET HEQET BES

For an Amulet of Protection:

DUA ANKH DJED WADJET NEITH

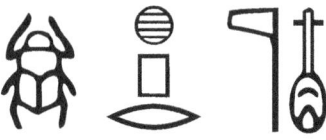

Kheper, the Scarab who pushes Ra's Boat in the sky.

For Protection *from* nefarious Demons or Akhu:

DUA IHY OSIRIS-NEBHOTEP DJOSER RA

For Protection *from* Evil Spirits:

DUA BES ANUBIS SET MAATI NEHEBU-KAU

For assembling an Army of Akhu (Angels):

DUA OSIRIS-RA AKHU-NEFERU NEITH

For attracting Police or Law Enforcement:

DUA HORUR NEKHA HOR BES

For attracting Soldiers, Military, or Emergency people:

DUA HORUR NEPHTHYS NEHEBU-KAU

For a Magic Circle of Protection (to be surrounded by a wall of Gravity that repels hostile Energies):

DUA KHONSU REN-SHEN MEH-URIT

To Protect Spells from disruption or being countered:

DUA HEKAU MU NI-ISFET

For summoning an Angel for one's defense:

DUA AKHU-NEFRU DI ANKH HOTEPU

Kheriheb Priest (Reader of the Sacred Text)

For Protection from reading Ancient Documents:

DUA SESHET THOTH ISIS-NEPHTHYS

To Protect your Friends, their Homes and their Families:

DUA SOBEK NEKHA PER-ANKH ANKHU

To Protect one's work or employment from interference / "Office Politics" or gossip / rumors / scandals / intrigue / drama:

DUA SESHET PER-ANKH ANKHU

To Protect yourself and a companion:

DUA SA-ANKH SA-REN THOTH PTAH-RA

To Protect your lover or mistress:

DUA HATHOR OSIRIS HEQET ANKH

For Protection from unseen illnesses or social conditions:

DUA THOTH SIA NEKHA MEHEN BES

For Protection from Religious Extremists:

DUA SA-ANKHU EM HEM-NETERU SENA

For Protection **from Idiots**:

DUA BES SA ANKH DI SEKHEM ANKH HOTEPU

To Protect

For Protection:

HAIL NEKHBET ASET UATCHET BES NUT FOREVER!

To Stop All Violence and Battles:

HAIL HORUS-OF-EDFU FOREVER!

To Stop all Pestilence and Diseases:

HAIL SAKHMET, QUEEN OF HEAVEN!

To Guard your Home or Residence:

HAIL HORUS SET ANUBIS THOTH SESHET FOREVER!

To Protect your Tomb or Gravesite:

HAIL AUSAR-OSIRIS, GIVEN LIFE FOREVER!

To Protect your Pets and Home:

HAIL BAST ANUBIS PER-AA ASET FOREVER!

To Protect all of your Possessions and Assets:

HAIL ANUBIS, GIVEN LIFE AND OFFERINGS!

To Protect a vehicle while in motion:

HAIL HORUS-OF-THE-SKY FOREVER!

To Protect the unborn:

HAIL BES, GIVER OF LIFE, FOREVER!

To Protect Children from Bullies:

HAIL HAROERIS THE VICTORIOUS FOREVER!

Bes is the Protector of Children and the Unborn. He also protects against Nightmares.

(Amulet)

To Stop Terrorism and Fear Mongering:

HAIL SET WHO GUARDS RA'S BOAT!

To Stop an Earthquake or Tsunami:

HAIL GEB OF THE EARTH, BELOVED OF SHU!

To Stop Rain or Floods:

HAIL TUTANKHAMON, SON OF RA, FOREVER!

To Stop a Prolonged Drought:

HAIL NU HAPY TEFNUT FOREVER!

To Stop Fierce or Strong Winds:

HAIL SHU AMUN, KING OF THE GODS!

To Stop Chaos or Mayhem or Riots:

HAIL MAAT MAATI, ORDER AND TRUTH!

To Stop Civil Unrest:

HAIL MAAT THOTH SESHET FOREVER!

To Protect a City or Town:

HAIL HORUS-SET, GOD OF PEACE!

To Protect Pyramids & Egyptian Temples:

HAIL CHEOPS-KHUFU KHAFRE MENKAURA DI ANKH PER ANKH DI ANKH SEKHEM HOTEPU EN MASRI EM ISFET NI ISFET ANKH

Chapter 5: Magical Self-Defense:

Medical-Healing:

Thoth the Thrice-Great (God of Medicine)

For Excellent Health and Well-Being:

DUA IMHOTEP DI-NEFERU-SONEB

To cure or cease common cold or Influenza viruses, or other Pestilences:

DUA SAKHMET ANKH

To heal stomach flu, indigestion, diarrhea, constipation or pain:

DUA DUAMUTEF NEITH ANKH

To treat liver, gall or spleen conditions:

DUA AMSETI ISIS ANKH

To heal a cough, (breathing) or congestion:

DUA HAPY NEPHTHYS ANKH

To heal colon or intestinal issues or pain:

DUA QEBEHSENWF SELQET ANKH

To cure any infection or injury:

DUA NEHMETAWY ISHTAR

To heal heart conditions or heal Cancer:

DUA KHEPERI ANKH

To cure dehydration:

DUA HAPY-NUN DI NW

"Recover from Sickness"

To repair bones, cells, tissues, fractures or heal sprained tendons:

DUA THOTH IMHOTEP DJED

To rejuvenate one's health:

DUA HARPOCRATES SONEB-NEFRU ARQU

To heal back injuries or alleviate pain:

DUA THOTH DJED-NEFRU SIA

To alleviate Depression or Sadness:

DUA BES IHY OSIRIS HORI-SA-UR

For a safe childbirth:

DUA BES LAT BAST MESKHENET TAURET

To cure dehydration, heat stroke or dry skin:

DUA AB-NUNU MERIT MU ANKH

To restore (resurrect) an **intact body** with its original soul and spirit (**if it is willing**):

DUA PTAH-OSIRIS-RA WADJET WEPWAWET ANKH-SHEN

[*Uses Telepathy + Chronokinesis*]

To stop any addictions:

DUA WERETHEKAU IMHOTEP ANKH

"Music, Joy, Happiness"

To heal acute blindness or other discomfort:

DUA WADJET SIA SHAI NEFERU-SONEB

For increased Fertility, sexual energy:

DUA HATHOR MIN QETESH BAST

For better performance (sexual energy):

DUA QETESH HEQET BABI MIN

For attraction of a Mate or Lover:

DUA HATHOR MIN BAST

To cure common Pestilence:

DUA THOTH SAKHMET

To cure bacterial infections or parasites:

DUA NEHMETAWY SAKHMET BES

For increased bravery or courage:

DUA HORUR BABI MEH-URIT NEFERTUM

For invisibility, illusion (*works at right-angles*):

DUA AMUN WADJET SIA

To relieve skin conditions, acne, blemishes:

DUA ISHTAR ARQU IMHOTEP SONEB-ANKH

"Imsety, one of the 4 Sons of Horus"

(Protector of the Liver)

To relieve bodily pains, headaches, or cramps:

DUA MAAT SIA IMHOTEP NEKHA

To control blood cells in healing an injury or repel a bacterial infection:

DUA UKHET-ET THOTH SENIB ARQU

To cure or relieve symptoms of Cancer:

DUA SAKHMET RA HOTEP

For relieving any illness or disease:

DUA IMHOTEP SAKHMET THOTH

For healing with Visions:

DUA WADJET SONEB-NEFRU HOTEP

To attract First Aid, Medicine, Bandages, Compresses, or Medication (Plants):

DUA RENENUTET TA-BIJET ISHTAR

To reduce the size of Tumors, Boils or Cysts:

DUA OSIRIS-KA MONTU SAKHMET HEH

To heal some forms of Blindness:

DUA WADJET DI ANKH URP-NFR HTP

Hapi (Son of Horus)

(Protector of Lungs)

To relieve heart or other organ diseases:

DUA KHEPERI MAAT AB-NEFRU IB-NEFRU

To treat heat stroke, dehydration, fainting, low blood sugar levels, and to prevent drowning:

DUA SHU HAPY AMAM DI HOTEPU NEFRU

To avoid thoughts leading to hallucination or false memories:

DUA THOTH SESHET MAATI DI ANKH HOTEP

To heal an injury with heat energy:

DUA SET HATHOR SAKHMET DI ANKH

To punish evil fingers touching one's body:

DUA APOPHIS ISIS SAA DI ANKH HOTEPU

To punish Evil Spirits who attack one's body:

DUA KAU NEFRU AKHU DI ANKH HOTEPU

To punish Evil People who attack one's body:

DUA KHAT NEFRU AKHU DI ANKH HOTEPU

To treat Water Intoxication:

DUA HAPY DI NATRON ANKH HOTEPU

For protection during Surgery:

DUA BES AKHU KAU DI ANKH HOTEPU

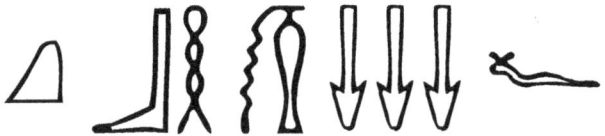

Qebehsenuef (Son of Horus)

(Protector of the Intestines)

To stop all illnesses or plagues:

HAIL THOTH IMHOTEP FOREVER!

To stop infections:

HAIL SESHET IMHOTEP, GIVEN OFFERINGS!

To heal injuries or cuts or open wounds:

HAIL SET, WHO GUARDS THE SKIN!

To heal internal problems, pain, or discomfort:

HAIL THOTH DUAMUTEF, FOREVER!

To stop Depressing Thoughts:

HAIL RA IN THE WINTER! HAIL BES IN THE SUMMER!

To inspire Creativity:

HAIL PTAH KHNUM FOREVER!

To request enlightenment and knowledge:

HAIL PTAH, HUSBAND OF SAKHMET, FOREVER!

To relieve Cancer symptoms:

HAIL SAKHMET AND RA FOREVER!

To relieve irritation and Diarrhea:

HAIL QEBEHSENWF AND SELQET FOREVER!

To cause tumors to shrivel up:

HAIL SET AND ISIS FOREVER!

(Duamutef, Son of Horus)

"He praises his mother"

(Protector of the Stomach)

To relieve bodily pains or symptoms:

HAIL HORUS AND HATHOR FOREVER!

To stop the symptoms of Colds or Influenza:

HAIL HORUS-THE-ELDER, GUARDIAN OF PEACE!

To stop symptoms of Gall or Kidney Stones:

HAIL DUAMUTEF AND ASET (ISIS) FOREVER!

To cure or treat dry skin:

HAIL HAPY SHU TEFNUT & SESHET FOREVER!

To prevent suicidal thoughts:

HAIL BES FOREVER!

To prevent a drug overdose:

HAIL SESHET THOTH IMHOTEP GIVEN LIFE!

To prevent dangerous behavior:

HAIL SET BES HAROERIS NEPHTHYS FOREVER!

To prevent sexually transmitted diseases:

HAIL MIN HATHOR HORUS BES FOREVER!

To prevent reckless behavior:

HAIL KHNUM NEPHTHYS PTAH FOREVER!

To heal Gout:

HAIL KHEPER SET NEPHTHYS GIVEN LIFE!

To attract First Aid, Bandages, ointments, compresses, and Medicine:

"Hail Imhotep and Thoth! May I receive medical treatment immediately. So declares Pharaoh M7, true of voice."

To Find a Cure to some illness or situation, social issue, or to Heal with Visions:

"Hail Wadjet Soneb Nefru Medat Hotep! May I find a solution to my problem. May I receive a vision from the Gods to resolve my situation. So declares Pharaoh M7, true of voice, living forever."

To cure Insomnia (sleeplessness):

"Hail Nephthys, Goddess of Night. May I sleep well, may I dream well, may nothing prevent me from sleeping. So declares Pharaoh M7, true of voice, living forever."

To prevent Sleep-walking:

DUA NEPHTHYS ISIS DI ANKH URP-NFR HTP

For General Excellent Health and Well Being:

"Hail Thoth, Imhotep, Seshet and Maat! May my body be healthy, vigorous, and strong. So declares Pharaoh M7, true of voice, living forever through Ma'at."

To stop indigestion or stomach pain:

"Hail Duamutef, Son of Horus! May my stomach not feel pain, may my food digest properly. May I have no more gas or discomfort. So declares Pharaoh M7, true of voice, living forever."

To cure Dehydration:

"O Hapy the Nile God, bestow upon me the Waters of Life, that I may drink from them."

To stop the effects of Hypnosis:

"O Thoth, may you interrupt the trance of the people by slashing water into their faces, or thrusting your lit torch to their eyes. So declares Pharaoh M7, true of voice, living forever."

Chapter 6: Counter Magic

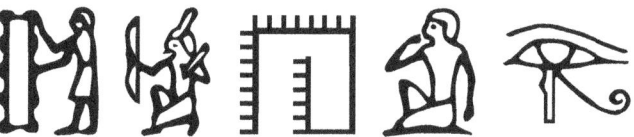

To return fire to an adversary who cast Magic against one; to Counter-attack:

DUA AM-HEH SAKHMET BES ANKH

To Curse an adversary with Frost & Fire:

DUA TEFNUT SAKHMET

To Curse an Enemy with Earthquakes:

DUA GEB ALDINACH PAKHET

To Curse an Enemy with Storms & Quakes:

DUA ALDINACH SET SAKHMET

To cause Rain:

DUA TEFNUT

To cause Hail or Snow:

DUA TEFNUT SHU

To cause Sunlight to appear from clouds:

DUA RA-HOR ATON

To cause wildfires:

DUA SAKHMET SHU

For revenge against some wrongdoing by an unknown adversary:

DUA HAROERIS ANAT MESKHENET SELQET

To cease wildfires:

DUA TEFNUT DI NW NI SAKHMET SHU

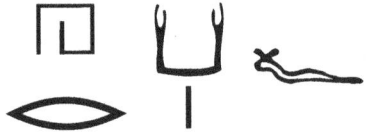

"He rests his Ka Spirit"

To settle differences and make amends:

DUA OSIRIS NEB-ANKH DI-HOTEP

To fill an Enemy with Love-Energy, and stop their aggression:

DUA HATHOR OSIRIS NAKHT

To curse & trace an unknown adversary's actions to their location:

DUA DJEHUTY MAAT SHAI

To trace an enemy's telephone line to their location and attack them:

DUA TUTANKHAMON M7 TUTU MAAHES

To counter attack any Cyber or Internet attack:

DUA NEBKHEPERURA THOTH SESHET HA MAFDET

To attack the Evil Arab-Terrorist States ("Islamic States" / "Caliphate"):

DUA APOPHIS SET SOPDU NEITH SELQET BES

To Prevent "Lone Wolf" attacks:

DUA ANUP SET ASARIS NI ISFET NI DI HOTEP

"To Curse my Enemies."

To bind any opposing sorcerers in a Triangle to prevent their actions from success:

DUA SEPED NAUNET RESHEF NEPHTHYS ANKH

To counter-attack those cursing you and to undo their Magic spells:

DUA THOTH HEKAU SESHET NI-MAAXORU

To conquer an Enemy or Rogue Nation:

DUA HOR SENIB-SENA SENERIT TAU

To conquer organized crime or gangs/Mafia:

DUA HOR ONURIS ANAT MAATI

To cause Islamic-Terrorists to be defeated or vanquished:

DUA HORUR HOR MIHOS SESMU KEK NI-ISFET

To cause Political adversaries to lose a battle:

DUA HOR M7 DI-SUKKA EM ISFET

To cause random events in the News:

DUA SHAI AGAB KHEPERI M7

To destroy an enemy stronghold

DUA SENIB-SENA SENAKHT ARTCHATU

"To have Power over, to seize."

To hinder sorcerers from operating:

DUA THOTH-AAU IMHOTEP PTAHHOTEP

To attack *your* archenemy:

DUA KHAT SET NEHEBU-KAU M7 MENHIT

To destroy *my* enemies completely:

DUA SOKARIS SESMU AMMOT RA-HOTEP M7

To send a Tsunami (*tidal wave caused by an undersea earthquake*) to a target:

DUA ALDINACH GEB NU SHU APOPHIS

To send a hurricane to a target:

DUA NU TEFNUT SHU AMUN AM-HEH EN SENA

To attack people *who wish to destroy our Monuments in Egypt*; to Protect Egypt from enemies:

DUA HORUR HEMT ABENEKA BAGASA TCHAT NI-AUR NI-MAAXORU EM ARAM

To cause some Wind:

DUA AMUN SHU HOTEP

To cause Arab-Spring Revolutions:

DUA MASR NI ISFET, DI ANKH NI HOTEP

"May the God give Wind to My Enemies."

To end Public Gossip or Rumors:

DUA MAAT NI-THET-THET

To stop all incoming Curses, Enchantment, Spells, Hexes, Jinxes, Exorcisms, Prayers, and Bindings:

HAIL HEKA GOD OF MAGIC, PROTECT ME, FOREVER!

To stop the Evil Eye from success:

HAIL WADJET EYE OF HORUS FOREVER!

To stop all Evil Magic from success:

HAIL HORUS-THE-BLIND, TURN AWAY YOUR ENEMY!

To stop all Hostile and Negative Energy from persisting:

HAIL RA ATON FOREVER!

To absorb all incoming Energy:

HAIL RA ATON, GIVEN LIFE AND OFFERINGS!

To combat all Hostile Magic approaching you:

HAIL SAKHMET RA SET HORUS SOBEK FOREVER!

To bind an enemy sorcerer to prevent success:

HAIL SHAI NEHEBKA WADJET ISIS FOREVER!

To remove the anger from a God or Goddess:

HAIL NETERU (NETJERU) NEFERU FOREVER!

"To repel Insects from invading our homes."

To summon Akhu from Heaven for one's defense:

HAIL THE IMMORTAL LEGIONS OF CAESAR-HORUS!

To create Earthquakes and other Plagues to an Enemy combatant:

HAIL GEB SAKHMET SHU AMUN TEFNUT FOREVER!

To cause Terrorists to be captured or arrested:

HAIL HORUS-OF-THE-HORIZON, GIVEN LIFE!

To cause Murderers and Thieves to be captured or arrested:

HAIL HORUS-OF-EDFU, GIVEN OFFERINGS!

To cause Gangs, Vandals, Drug-dealers, Arsonists, and other illegal groups to be arrested:

HAIL HORUS-OF-GOLD, THE CONQUEROR, FOREVER!

To stop Computer Viruses from continuing:

HAIL HORUS, SLAYER OF APOPHIS, FOREVER!

Using a cellular phone, <u>visualize</u> the person talking to you and *break their neck* in the vision <u>if they are Enemies of Pharaoh</u>:

HAIL HORUR AA NETER AA DI ANKH URP NEFRU

Call a cell phone with Telepathy:

HAIL M7-HORUR AA TEP DI ANKH HOTEPU

"To Remove, or put aside."

To Liberate & Avenge Ancient Palmyra from ISIS* Terrorists:

DUA AMONRA NU TEFNUT SHU APOPHIS SET SAKHMET PALMYRA DI-ANKH MAAT HOTEP

To Destroy ISIS-Terrorist Sleeper-Cells World-Wide:

DUA HORU NEPHTHYS AMMOT HOTEP DI-ANKH MAAT DJED WAS SAKHEM

To Destroy all Funding for ISIS and Other Terrorism Groups World-wide:

DUA AMUNRA AST SESHET NEITH SELQET DI-ANKH

To Convert Sunni Arabs to Egyptian Belief Systems:

DUA M7-HORU HOTEP DI-MAAT

To Conquer Monotheism and Cause Horus Michael to rule the world as is his Birthright:

DUA M7-HORU KA-NAKHT BU PERO EM TAU

To Liberate Earth from the Caliphate and its followers:

DUA ISIS NI ARAM, DI HOTEP ANKH, NI ISFET

(ISIS = Islamic State of Iraq & Syria, ©2014CE)

Counter-Terrorism

Liberation of Iraq & Syria from ISIS Group:

To Liberate Ramadi from ISIS Terrorists:

DUA AMUNRA MONTU HORU SET DI-ANKH RAMADI

To Liberate Falluja from ISIS Terrorists:

DUA AMUNRA FALLUJA MONTU HORU SET DI-ANKH

To Liberate Mosul from ISIS Terrorists:

DUA AMUNRA IESU MOSUL HORU SET DI-ANKH

To Liberate Tikrit from ISIS Terrorists:

DUA AMUNRA TIKRIT MONTU HORU SET NEITH DI-ANKH

To Liberate Kirkuk from ISIS Terrorists:

DUA AMUNRA NEITH SELQET KIRKUK AST DI-ANKH

To Liberate Hawija from ISIS Terrorists:

DUA AMUNRA AST NEITH NEPHTHYS HAWIJA HORU DI-ANKH

To Liberate Samarra from ISIS Terrorists:

DUA AMONRA NEITH SAMARRA BES DI-ANKH

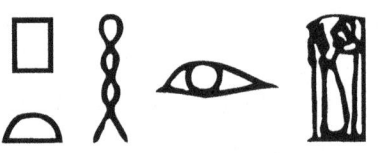

The Creator, Pt-h (Ptah)

To Liberate Aleppo from ISIS Terrorists:

DUA AMUNRA SAKHMET SET ALEPPO DI-ANKH

To Liberate Raqqa from ISIS Terrorists:

DUA AMONRA NEBKHEPERURA SET RAQQA DI-ANKH

To Liberate Deir Al-Zour from ISIS Terrorists:

DUA AMONRA SOBEK NEITH DEIR-AL-ZOUR NETERU-AA DI-ANKH

To Liberate Anbar Province from ISIS Terrorists:

DUA AMONRA SAKHMET SET NEITH SOBEK ANBAR DI-ANKH

To Liberate Abu Kamal from ISIS Terrorists:

DUA AMONRA APOPHIS HORU ABU-KAMAL DI-ANKH MAAT HEH

To Liberate Hasaka from ISIS Terrorists:

DUA AMONRA SET NEPHTHYS HASAKA DI-ANKH

To Liberate Kobani from ISIS Terrorists:

DUA AMONRA HOTEP KOBANI DI-ANKH

To Dispel or Reflect Magic sent against Me (or You):

DUA HATHOR ANKH ZESSET DI HOTEP

To take away all powers (Energy) and strength of My Enemy (or your adversary), to cause them fatigue, and prevent them from taking actions:

DUA AA-NETER DI KAU UAS DI HOTEP

To Become Invisible or Translucent so one's adversary cannot see you (as Protection):

DUA AMONRA DI ANKH ES MAAT HOTEP

For acquiring Amulets & Talisman Charms:

DUA THOTH DI TET HEKAU SHEN

For protecting one's car or vehicle from Birds or rocks:

DUA HOR-RA ASARIS DI HOTEP

To Give Protection from all Hostile Magic or Energy:

DUA RA AA NAKHT AR-NEFRU NI SAKHEM HEKAU

To stop all Curses from Effect:

DUA THOTH RA PTAH AMUN EM HOTEP DI ANKH URP-NEFRU

To stop all Evil Magic from Effect:

DUA RA ATUM AA NI ISFET SAKHEM

To Prevent Sorcerers from Operating:

DUA RA MAAHRU NI HEKAU KAU

To remove the Ka Energy from an aggressor (*Causes Fatigue*):

DUA NETER KA EM RA AA NI ISFET KAU

To prevent foreign Mages from working Black Magic:

ARNKHY HOR M7 EM ISFET HEKAU

For Divine Protection at home or when traveling (via Angels, etc.):

DUA AKHU NEFRU NETRU DI HOTEP

For Protection of one's home, possessions, pets, assets, jobs, investments, lifestyle, vehicles, friends, and family:

DUA ANKHU PER-ANKH MAHIU AKHU DI HOTEP

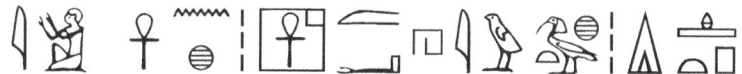

To attract Security Guards, Police, Doctors, Nurses, Paramedics, Life Guards, Soldiers, etc.:

DUA HOR NETRU-NEFRU DI HOTEP

To Protect one's home, pets, friends, job, and medical coverage from being disturbed:

DUA ASAR PER-ANKH ARNKY BAST ANUP THOTH HOTEP

For immediate Protection:

DUA HORUR EM HOTEP

For protecting assets overseas:

DUA NU HOR ARNKHY HOTEP

To attract Soldiers, Policemen, Firemen, or Doctors:

DUA HOR THOTH RA EM HOTEP

To attract Lifeguards, Nurses, Paramedics, etc.:

DUA THOTH IMHOTEP HOR EM HOTEP

For protection from Insects or Animals:

DUA BES SOBEK ASARIS HOTEP

For protection from or avoiding poisonous creatures:

DUA SERQET ARNKHY NEITH AST HEH

For protection from thieves, vandals, rioters, or other criminal persons:

ARNKHY PER-ANKH AAKH-ETU EM ISFET

For protection from Mentally Unstable People:

DUA THOTH IMHOTEP TEP NEFERU HOTEP

To Protect Animals or pets from danger or harm:

DUA BAST ANUB SOBEK ARNKHY ANKHU HOTEP

To Protect Government Officials or Kings (etc.):

DUA PERAA MAAHRU DI TET HEH HOTEP

To Protect a City from harm:

DUA HOR ASARIS NI ISFET

To Protect Egypt from Terrorism:

DUA PTAH ARNKHY TAU EM ISFET

To protect your Country from Terrorism:

DUA ASARIS-RA MAAHRU NI ISFET

To Protect your family & home from Terrorism:

DUA AST BAST SERQET EM ISFET

To Protect your friends & their families from Terrorism:

DUA AST SERQET ARNKHY ANKHU EM ISFET HEH

For protection from wild animals or foreign diseases <u>and Epidemics</u>:

DUA SAKHMET SOBEK ANUP EM HOTEP

To protect tombs:

DUA PER-HEH ARNKHY EM ISFET

To Protect children from bullies and weapon access:

DUA HORU ASARIS AST DI TET WADJET HOTEP

To Protect newly born children:

DUA BES NEFRU EM HOTEP

For a Safe Childbirth:

DUA BES MUT TAURET NEKHBET DI ANKH URP

Chapter 7: Counter-Offensive: City Spells

To cause a Budget Surplus in a City or State:

AR NUB HEDU MONETA AMONRA HOTEP!

For increased Revenues, Tax Collections, or earnings from exports:

AR KHERI-A NEFERU UPI SHEN!

To reduce Crime in a City:

AR KAF KHBENET, DUA MAAT MAXXORU!

To stop or prevent Vandalism, Riots, or social issues:

DUA MAAT MAAXORU!

To create well-paying jobs, employment, or work for your citizens:

DUA SHAI HORU MONETA MAAXORU!

To stop wildfires, floods, or mayhem:

DUA HAPY, DUA SAKHMET NEFERU HOTEP!

To Collect Taxes, Tariffs, or other Revenue:

DUA MONETA NEFERU HOTEP HEH!

To stop social problems:

DUA MAATI HORU THOTH!

To prevent or Cease Shootings, Mass Panic, or Terrorism:

DUA MONTU HORU AMON HOTEP!

For Law-Abiding Citizens:

DUA HORU MAAT!

For non-oppressive Legislation:

DUA MAAT MAATI THOTH DJED!

For Fairness in Law and Order:

DUA NEFERU MAATI!

For General Happiness and Prosperity:

DUA NEFERU DJA HOTEP!

To inspire Creativity:

DUA ATUM PTAH HOTEP!

Weather:

Amon the Wind God

(Amen, Amun, Amonou, Imin)

To cause Rain:

HAIL TEFNUT, GODDESS OF MOISTURE!

To cause Morning Dew or Humidity:

HAIL TEFNUT AND SHU, THE DIVINE TWINS!

To cause Snow:

HAIL TEFNUT, COLD OF WINTER!

To cause Wind Gusts:

HAIL AMUN AND SHU, GIVEN OFFERINGS!

To cause a Clear Sky with Sunshine:

HAIL RA, THE GREAT SOLAR GOD!

To cause a Rainbow:

HAIL AMONRA TEFNUT AND SHU!

To cause overcast Clouds:

HAIL TEFNUT, LADY OF GRAY!

To cause the Sun to open in the sky:

HAIL PTAH, THE OPENER OF WAYS!

To cause Floods:

HAIL TEFNUT, YOUR CHILD HAS RED HAIR!

To make peace with the Gods:

HAIL THE NETERU (NETJERU), GIVEN OFFERINGS!

Ra, the Solar God

To undo any Magic:

HAIL HORUS-MICHAEL, GOD OF WEALTH!

To cause the sky to rain down Frogs:

HAIL HEKET, THE FROG GODDESS!

For Silence in the Sky:

HAIL HARPOCRATES FOREVER!

For a Solar Heat wave:

HAIL AMONRA AND SHU FOREVER!

For mild weather:

HAIL RA TEFNUT HORUS, GIVEN OFFERINGS!

To Stop Erosion:

HAIL GEB AND TEFNUT FOREVER!

For clear-air turbulence:

DUA SHU AA AMON AA

To stop clear-air turbulence

DUA SHU AMON NI AA DI HOTEP

Governing Spells:

Osiris, Lord and Judge of the Living.

To prevent *accidental* Copyright Infringement or Plagiarism:

DUA THOTH HOTEP SESHAT TEP

To prevent theft of all kinds:

DUA ANUBIS DI-AUAU XA

To prevent vandalism or damage to property:

DUA HORUR NI-AUR AUAU

To prevent Cyber stalking or bullying:

DUA THOTH SET HOTEP

To prevent provocation of any crime:

DUA MAAT MAATI HOTEP BES

To prevent libel, slander, insults:

DUA SESHAT IMHOTEP HU DI-HOTEP

To stop Gossip or Rumors:

DUA THOTH NI-THETTHET XA

To prevent trespassing and invasion of privacy:

DUA AKHU KHAT NEITH PER-ANKH

Osiris (Asar)

To prevent home invasion, robbery, or intrusion:

DUA BAST NEITH ISIS PER NI-AUAU

To prevent offending foreign religions or social ideas from libel in the media:

DUA HORU TEP SESHAT NI-NETER HEB

To prevent American Freedoms from infringing on the rights of society in the rest of the World:

DUA GEB ANKHU MAAT NI-SENA HEH

To stop training for terrorists, extremists, political cults, criminals, or other groups:

DUA HORU GEB MAAT NI-SENA XA

To stop misuse of technology:

DUA THOTH ASAR HOTEP

To stop spies from stealing data:

DUA SESHAT HOTEP NEKHA

To prevent or stop harassment of all kinds:

DUA TEP HATHOR-MIN HOTEP

Maat, Goddess of Justice, Truth, Law & Order, Stability, Honesty, and Cosmic Balance.

To prevent or stop destruction of property:

DUA SET DI-PER-ANKH SEN-B

To find suspects in a criminal or civil investigation:

DUA THESU HORI-SA-UR MAAT

To collect and find evidence of a crime:

DUA THOTH HOR NI-KHEBENT

To find hidden information:

DUA SESHAT THOTH IMHOTEP

To capture a wanted fugitive:

DUA SET HORU HOTEP

To capture terrorists:

DUA HORU DI-KHEBETY XA

To prevent terrorists from destroying property, monuments, relics, or buildings:

DUA HORU DI-KHEBETY HEH

To capture or arrest terrorist leaders:

DUA SET APOPHIS DI-ARAM XA

Maati, Goddess of the Scales

To prevent firearms from accidental discharge or firing:

DUA SET HORU DI-KHEFA PET

To prevent hidden explosives from activation or detonation:

DUA SET NI-PET KHEFA

To prevent people with Mental Illnesses from interfering with society, or causing crimes:

DUA TEP THOTH NI-HEGI

To calm violent people in a situation:

DUA HORU DI-HOTEP PAX IHY

To calm or prevent riots:

DUA HORU-MAAT PAX NI-BAGASA

To prevent killing or armed robbery:

DUA HORU SA ANKHU NI-SENA

To capture or subdue Murderers or Assassins:

DUA HORU S-NEHET SENA XA

To capture thieves of all kinds:

DUA HORU-ANUBIS DI-AUAU XA

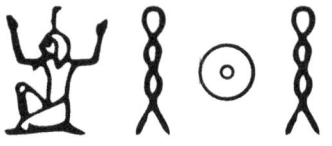

Heh, God of Eternity

To capture *terrorists, arsonists, vandals, murderers, hate-crime suspects, cyber or technology violators, bullies and gangsters, drug dealers,* **or other criminals**:

DUA MAATI DI-AUR AUAU SENA XA

To capture rapists:

DUA SET MIN HOTEP NI-AUR

To prevent officers from firing on innocent people:

DUA HORU SET MAAT NI-HEM KHEFA

To prevent officers from accidentally shooting or attacking innocent people who resemble the guilty (i.e. skin color, clothing, etc.):

DUA MAAT THOTH HOTEP

To summon Back Up or Auxiliaries:

DUA HORU DI-AUTCHARU XA

To prevent Cars or vehicles from speeding (faster than posted limit):

DUA PAX-MAATI WORRET

To prevent cars from running through a traffic stop or yield sign or red light:

DUA MAATI-WORRET NI-IWA

Sakhmet, Goddess of Plagues, Diseases, Healing, War, Fire, and Powers.

To prevent collisions, bumper violations, or hit-and-run events:

DUA HESPU SEBAI MAAT

To prevent reckless driving and legal impairment or distractions:

DUA SEBAI MAAT BES HOTEP

To prevent car crashes from distractions:

DUA MAATI HOTEP

To prevent or stop cars from cutting in front of your traffic lane:

DUA ANUBIS MAAT SEBAI HESPU

To prevent drivers from not using signaling when changing lanes (to cause drivers to signal when moving):

DUA GEB MAATI PAX BES HOTEP

To cease or prevent Road Rage:

DUA HORU NI-SET HOTEP

For not blasting one's horn unnecessarily:

DUA SOBEK IHY HOTEP

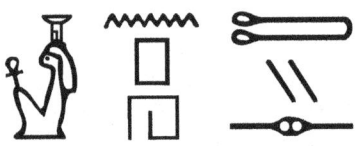

Nephthys, Goddess of the Pharaohs and of Nighttime.

For illegal use of parking with a Permit or legal placard when **not disabled**:

DUA MIN WORRET MAATI

For preventing misuse of handicap or other placard (i.e. using it when not handicapped):

DUA MAAT KHEPERI MAATI MEDIT

To prevent or stop Double-Parking (parking alongside another already parked car):

DUA WORRET-HORU MAATI

For protecting pedestrians and Bikes:

SA IWA WORRETU DUA BES MAATI

To cause people to understand and comply with Traffic Laws and rules:

DUA THOTH MEDIT MAAT MAATI

For protecting ones "right of way":

DUA HORUR DI-ANKH BES RAHOTEP

For protecting animals from becoming road-kill on public or private roads:

DUA ANUBIS BAST HORU BES SA HEH

Khnum, a Creator God who fashioned Humans on his Pottery Wheel.

To prevent Drunk-Driving or driving while under the influence of drugs, technology, social issues, music, communications or other distractions:

DUA ASAR SA ANKHU DI-ANKH NI-URP

To maintain Social Order and Law Maintenance:

DUA MAAT SA GEB SA ANKHU

To prevent pollution on public roads:

DUA WAB ANKHU SA GEB

To punish with Divine Energy all violators of Traffic Laws & Red-Light Violators:

DUA SAKHMET SA MAAT MAATI PAX

To cause a Budget Surplus in a City or State:

AR NUB HEDU MONETA AMONRA HOTEP!

For increased Revenues, Tax Collections, or earnings from exports:

AR KHERI-A NEFERU UPI SHEN!

To reduce Crime in a City:

AR KAF KHBENET, DUA MAAT MAAHRU!

Bastet (Lady Bast), the Cat Goddess, Patron of the Home, Music, Dancing and Protection.

To stop or prevent Vandalism, Riots, or social issues:

DUA MAAT MAAXORU!

To create well-paying jobs, employment, or work for your citizens:

DUA SHAI HORU MONETA MAAXORU!

To stop wildfires, floods, or mayhem:

DUA HAPY, DUA SAKHMET NEFERU HOTEP!

To Collect Taxes, Tariffs, or other Revenue:

DUA MONETA NEFERU HOTEP HEH!

To stop social problems:

DUA MAATI HORU THOTH!

To prevent & Cease All Shootings, Mass Panic, or Terrorism:

DUA MONTU HORU AMON HOTEP!

For Law-Abiding Citizens:

DUA HORU MAAT!

For non-oppressive Legislation:

DUA MAAT MAATI THOTH DJED!

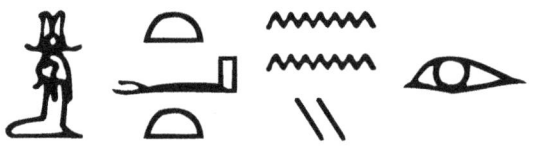

Tatenen, a Creator God

For Fairness in Law and Order:

DUA NEFERU MAATI!

For General Happiness and Prosperity:

DUA NEFERU DJA HOTEP!

To inspire Creativity:

DUA ATUM PTAH HOTEP!

For Good Luck (Chi Energy):

HAIL RA ATON GIVEN LIFE AND OFFERINGS FOREVER!

For a regional Peace:

HAIL OSIRIS GOD OF PEACE, MAY HE BE VICTORIOUS FOREVER!

For compassion of people:

HAIL HATHOR ISIS OSIRIS FOREVER!

To forgive all past actions and debts:

HAIL OSIRIS, WHO FORGIVES SET!

To end a War or Siege:

HAIL OSIRIS HORUS SET BES NEKHEN!

To end Terrorism wars:

HAIL THE GODDESS ISIS FOREVER!

Min, God of Fertility & Reproduction

To attract the opposite Gender in love:

HAIL HATHOR (HORUS) FOREVER!

To attract a young Maiden:

HAIL HATHOR FOREVER!

To attract peaceful thoughts and ideas:

HAIL PTAH AMON RA THOTH IMHOTEP FOREVER!

For a Truce, Cease-fire agreement or treaty:

HAIL MONTU AMON SET HORUS FOREVER!

To stop immediately all Hostility and Fighting or Arguing:

HAIL PTAH OSIRIS HORUS FOREVER!

To maintain Just Laws and Order:

HAIL MAAT, DAUGHTER OF RA, FOREVER!

To stop all riots and chaos (Isfet):

MAY HORUS BE FOREVER VICTORIOUS OVER ISFET!

To make Just and Reasonable Laws:

HAIL MAAT OF THE DOUBLE SCALE FOREVER!

To maintain Order, Justice, Tranquility and Honesty in Society:

HAIL PHARAOH HORUS-MICHAEL, GIVEN LIFE AND OFFERINGS FOREVER!

Hathor, Goddess of Love.

For your beloved to be attracted to you:

HAIL HATHOR HORUS BES OSIRIS FOREVER!

For angry people to be filled with love suddenly and without explanation:

HAIL HATHOR HORUR SET ASARIS DI HOTEP DI MRY

For people with hatred to suddenly become loving and caring:

HAIL HATHOR ASARIS SELQET SESHAT DI MRY ANKH NEFERU EM HOTEP DI ANKH HOTEPU

For people to <u>not</u> want to have sexual relations with strangers <u>nor</u> commit rape or sexual assault, ever:

HAIL HATHOR NI MIN ANKH NI TEP MIN ANKH

To stop rape and sexual assault:

HAIL AMON MIN HATHOR NI MIN ANKH NI HU ANKH

To increase fertility:

HAIL MIN EM HOTEP DI ANKH AA SAKHEM KAU AMON

To become friends with someone:

HAIL NEFERTUM DI ANKH HOTEPU NEFRU DI SESHEN

Weather Manipulation

(To Hostile Targets):

"**For causing rain**, cure a drought, cause Frogs to fall from the sky, or to cause flash floods to an enemy target: 'Hail Tefnut the Great! Open the flood gates over Seb! Rejoice, O Netrut!'"

"**For causing icy weather**, snow, blizzards, hail, cold fronts, hot hail (volcanic ash), cold air, or mudslides to an enemy: 'Hail Tefnut and Shu! Behold, I carry your child, and he has red hair!'"

"**For causing fires** to break out in an enemy target, for solar flares, wildfires, forest fires, heat, hot air, hot temperatures, or drought to an enemy target: 'Hail Sakhmet! I am Nefertum your son; I am being scolded by Seb, and require your aid.'"

"**For earthquakes** or mudslides to occur to an enemy target; or sink holes, avalanches, quicksand, or heavy rain to an enemy: 'Hail Seb, O Neter of the Earth! Send my enemy some movements!'"

"**For Tsunamis** to an enemy (tidal waves caused by a sea earthquake): 'Hail Nu, O Ocean of Creation!'"

"**For hurricanes**, Typhoons, tornadoes, water spouts, gale force winds, turbulence, sand storms, dust storms, or thunder and lightning to My Enemy: 'Hail Seth, O Neter of Chaos!'"

"**For a Clear Sky**: 'Hail Horus, Neter of the Sky, O One who is always Victorious!'"

Spell 1: To cause Rain:

DUA TEFNUT DI ANKH ES NEFER HOTEP

Spell 2: To cause Flooding:

DUA TEFNUT DI ANKH PER-THRW NUB BAS HOTEP

Spell 3: To cause Sinkholes (from Floods):

DUA TEFNUT NU GEB DI ANKH HEH

Spell 4: To cause Mudslides (from Floods):

DUA TEFNUT GEB HAPY ANKH HEH

Spell 5: To cause avalanches (from Erosion):

DUA GEB TEFNUT HOTEP

Spell 6: To cause Snow:

DUA TEFNUT NI RA

Spell 7: To cause Morning Dew:

DUA TEFNUT HOTEP

Spell 8: To cause a light drizzle of rain:

DUA TEFNUT ANKH

Spell 9: To cause Hail:

DUA TEFNUT AMUN HOTEP

Spell 10: To cause Sleet or Icy Roads:

DUA TEFNUT GEB EM HOTEP

Spell 11: To cause Dry Lightning:

DUA SHU SETH HOTEP

Spell 12: To cause normal Lightning:

DUA SETH SAKHEM HOTEP

Spell 13: To cause Thunder:

DUA SETH HOTEP

Spell 14: To cause a Storm:

DUA SETH TEFNUT SHU HOTEP

Spell 15: To cause Wind:

DUA AMUN HOTEP

Spell 16: To cause Strong Winds:

DUA AMUN NI HOTEP

Spell 17: To cause Dry Winds or Frogs:

DUA SHU HOTEP / DUA HEQET HOTEP

Spell 18: To cause Gale force Winds:

DUA AMUN AA NEB TAU HOTEP

Spell 19: To cause Still Atmosphere (Clear Sky):

DUA HOTEP EM HOTEP

Spell 20: To cause Hot Hail or Ash (Volcano eruption):

DUA GEB AA EM HOTEP

Spell 21: To cause Snow Storms or Blizzards:

DUA TEFNUT AMUN NI RA

Spell 22: To cause Tornadoes:

DUA SHU AMUN HOTEP

Spell 23: To cause Hurricanes or Darkness:

DUA SHU AMUN TEFNUT HOTEP / DUA APOPHIS HOTEP

Spell 24: To cause Solar Flares:

DUA RA HOTEP

Spell 25: To cause Solar Flame or Storms:

DUA RA SAKHMET HOTEP

Spell 26: To cause Dry Heat:

DUA SHU HOTEP

Spell 27: To cause a slight Drought:

DUA RA AA HOTEP

Spell 28: To cause Sunburn or Sunstroke:

DUA RA EM HOTEP

Spell 29: To cause small Earthquakes:

DUA GEB EM HOTEP

Spell 30: To cause Tsunamis (Earthquake caused tidal waves):

DUA GEB AA NU HOTEP

For causing Rain Only:

DUA TEFNUT, NETERT EN NUNUN!

For causing Rain or Fog:

DUA TEFNUT, DI AB NUNUN!

For causing Rain to cure a Drought; Floods, etc.:

DUA TEFNUT, DI AB NUNUN NI HKHST.

For causing Fog:

DUA TEFNUT NETERT, AR-PET NEFWU!

For causing Wind:

DUA SHU NETER, HEQA NEFWU DI ANKH-PERTXRU

For causing Strong Winds, Tornadoes, Water spouts, or Hurricanes::

DUA AMUN NETER, HEQA NEFWU AA!

<u>To Clear all Weather spells</u>, or undo any Weather whatsoever:

DUA PTAH AR, MERY DJEHUTI, DI ANKH MAAT!

For causing Storms, Lightning, Sandstorms, Tornadoes, etc.:

DUA SETH, HEQA ISFET, DI PERT-XRU!

For causing Earthquakes, Mudslides, Sinkholes, etc.:

DUA SETH, DUA GEB HEQA-TAU!

For causing small Earthquakes:

DUA GEB HEQA-TAU!

For Causing Hail, Sleet, Snow or Icy Weather:

DUA TEFNUT, AB-TAU SAKHEM!

To cause the sky to rain down Frogs:

DUA HEQT, NETERT EN WHAM-ANKH XA!

For Wildfires, Solar Flares, Dryness or Heat:

DUA SAKMET, DUA SHU, HEQA ZEMN!

For a Tsunami (*Tidal Wave caused by an Earthquake at Sea*):

DUA GEB, HEQA TAU IWAU NUNUN!

For Hot Hail (Volcanic Ash), Volcanic eruptions, or slope movements:

DUA GEB, HEQA PET-ZMN-XAST!

For a gentle breeze of air:

DUA AMUN HTP

For causing River water to appear like blood (*Red Algae Bloom*):

DUA HAPY, SA EN ASTES TET2, NUNUN!

To Part the Seas (with Wind or Water Spout):

DUA HAPY, XRP2-MW-Z4A!

For causing Acid Rain, Smog, or Black Hail:

DUA TEFNUT-SETH, DI ANKH!

For High Tides, Low Tides, or Great Tides: (?)

DUA HAPY, DUA AHY, DUA THOTH!

For an unusual Eclipse: (?)

DUA THOTH, DUA AHY HOTEP!

For Darkness, Clouds, or Haze:

DUA APOPHIS!

For a Torrential Flood:

DUA TEFNUT, DUA SETH, DUA NUNU!

For Sunny Weather, Clear Sky, and no Clouds:

DUA RA MAAHRU, DUA HORU HOTEP!

For Calm Seas:

DUA SHU HOTEP!

For a Rainbow after a Storm:

DUA RA HOTEP, MERY TEFNUT!

For a Fire Wall or Enclosure of Flame:

DUA SAKHMET, QAD ZAMEN!

For Ice Walls, or Snow:

DUA TEFNUT, DUA NUT, DUA AB-NEFER!

For Dry Lightning:

DUA SETH, DUA HORU!

For a Plague of Locusts <u>or other Insects</u>:

DUA BITY, DUA HORU, DUA HEQET!

For Boils on Enemy Targets:

DUA SAKHMET!

For "Bomb-Cyclones":

DUA SAKHMET SET TEFNUT NUT DI ANKH URP

For restoring Polar Ice:

DUA TEFNUT DI URP NEFERU TA HEH

For Gale-Force Winds to Hostile Targets:

DUA NEBKHEPERURA KA NAKHT TUT MESU

For Snow in Egypt:

DUA ATONRA TEFNUT DI NU

For Fire Tornadoes: (Pillar of Flame):

DUA SHU SET DI ANKH HTPW MAAHRU

To stop Glacier Melting:

DUA TEFNUT SET TAURET DI ANKH URP-NFR

To stop all Weather Plagues:

DUA HORU NI SAKHMET HTP

To stop all Pestilence Epidemics from spreading:

DUA SAU-HORU NI SAKHMET HTP

To end Climate Changes:

DUA PET-EM-HORU HTP, DUA NWT NFR HTP

For Mild Weather:

DUA HORU NI SET, DUA HTP DI ANKH

For a Clear Sky with Sunlight:

DUA RA AA EM HTP

Chapter 8: Counter-Politics:

For an Enemy to experience unnecessary Litigation & Civil Suits:

AMMOT THOTH HEH SESHET

For an Enemy to be inundated by Frogs, Locusts, Flies, Insects, or Rats:

HEQET SOBEK SHU

For an Enemy to be swarmed by honeybees, wasps, yellow jackets, or hornets:

BITY SHU SAKHMET

For an Enemy to be cursed with Love, and for Adulteries in General:

HATHOR ISIS SELQET

For an Enemy to become infertile:

MIN MONTU NEITH NI AMUN

For an Enemy to become ravenous with lust:

HATHOR SELQET HORUR

For an Enemy who attacks you with Magic, to become envious of his children or friends.

HEKAU TUT MERYT ATON

For an Enemy who curses Pharaoh with Magic, to feel hot and cold at the same time:

RA ATON SAKHMET SHU TEFFNUT

For an Enemy who dispels or reflects this Magic Book onto its author, to be smitten with Love by strangers:

HATHOR-7 APIS PTAH HEKAU MERY

For an Enemy who attacks the author, to feel as if being trampled upon:

HARMAKHIS PERO TUT USERMAATRA

For an Enemy who uses my Magic against me or my family or friends or pets or possessions or homes or cities (etc.), May the Enemy experience severe headaches or a fever:

HEKAU SAKHMET RA TEP AMUN HOTEP

For an Enemy who curses with illness to my Family, May the Enemy fall down and worship me as God, and break a bone in the process:

HEKAU DJED ASARIS SAKHMET NI MAAXORU

For an Enemy who won't go away, to cause the Enemy to feel afraid of you every time the Enemy sees you:

NEITH BES RA ANUBIS SETH MONTU

For an Enemy who seeks to claim your assets via a frivolous lawsuit, May that Enemy be sued for Perjury or fail in his/her attempts:

TOTH ANUBIS HORUR MAAT MAATI NEITH

For an Enemy who attacks you but will not parley with you, May that Enemy fail in his/her assaults:

SETH MAAT HORU MAATI NI MAAXORU

For an Enemy who wants or envies your possessions, May the Enemy be arrested for a trivial matter:

SETH MAATI ANUBIS THOTH BES AMUN

For an Enemy who investigates you for entertainment, May the Enemy become sick with Pestilence:

SAKHMET PTAH RA ATUM

For an Enemy who gossips about you, May the Enemy become embarrassed:

BES NEITH ISIS NEPHTHYS MONTU

For an Enemy who steals personal information about you, May the Enemy have heart disease:

KHEPERI NEITH BES SESHET

For an Enemy who spreads malicious rumors, May the Enemy experience sudden Influenza:

SAKHMET IMHOTEP AKH SESHET

For an Enemy who falsely accused you in a Court of Law: May the Court find the Enemy in Contempt of Court:

THOTH ANUBIS BES NEITH SOBEK

For an Enemy who attacks you with sharp fingers via Telepathy, May the Enemy become injured in an accident:

SELQET NEITH MONTU HOTEP

For an Enemy who kills your friends or relatives with Dark Magic, May the Enemy die in a fire:

SAKHMET SETH APOPHIS RA SOKAR

For an Enemy who desecrates Pharaoh's Family tombs, May the Enemy be deprived of an Afterlife in Duat or Heaven:

OSIRIS HORUR SETH PERO DUAT HOTEP

Healing & Success Spells:

To dispel all bodily Pains, migraine headaches, organ pain or discomfort:

DUA DUAMUTEF HAPY QEBEHSENWF IMSETY

To relieve a pinched nerve in the spine:

NEFRU-DJED NEFERU SONEB TEP MAAXORU

For your sports team to win the MLB World Series:

DUA PER-ANKH SETEM KAU NEFRU

For a solution to a problem:

DUA M7 MAAXORU HOTEP

To rejuvenate one's body; restore its integrity:

DUA KHNUM HOTEP SONEB HOTEP NEFRU

To acquire Psychic Energy to work Magic:

DUA MANA CHI SAKHEM PU HOTEP

To prevent Psychic Energy Overload:

DUA SAKHEM HOTEP

For your team to win the Super-Bowl football game:

DUA PER-ANKH NEBK SENET MAAHRU

For your Sports Team to win:

DUA PER-ANKH SENET XA MAAHRU

For your gambling team to win a contest:

DUA PER-ANKH SENET HEH MAAHRU

To acquire winnings from a contest:

DUA WADJET NUBSENU DI HEH NUB

For acquiring winning numbers in a lottery:

DUA SHAI WADJET DI MAAHRU HEH

Conquest Magic 2

To Conquer or defeat Islamic Terrorists:

DUA MONTU AMUN NI ARAM ISLAMI

To Destroy Terrorism Weapons:

DUA SELQET NEITH MONTU ANKH

To Capture Terrorist Soldiers:

DUA NEITH HORUR ARAM AL-QAEDA

To Overthrow a Caliphate:

DUA AMONRA AMONKA HOTEP

To Capture the Caliph:

KHEFA KALIPHA IBRAHIM, NI MAAXORU

To Find Terrorist Weapons on Vehicles:

KHEFA HEGI EM ARTCHATU AHA-T

To detect hidden information, secrets:

KHEFA ARAM PAPYRI AMUN

To destroy Islamic Terrorist Leaders:

DUA SETH HORUR NI ARAM AL-QAEDA

To capture Anarchists or Anti-Government:

KHEFA SETHIU KHARU PETTIU KHENTIU

To capture Vandals, Arsonists, or Rioters:

DUA HORUR NEITH SELQET MAAXORU

To capture Murderers and Assassins:

KHEFA JIHADIS ISFET NINJAS

To disable Bombs or IED weapons:

KHEFA KHEPESHU JIHADIS

To prevent Terrorism Assaults:

SENIB S-NEHET AL-QAEDA ARAM

To Conquer a Terrorist Caliphate:

SENIB SNA ARAM AL-QAEDA KHALIFATE

To Defend Egypt from Religious Terrorism:

SENIB MASR KMT EM JIHADIS ARAM AL-QAEDA

To Defend Egypt from Riots and other Evils:

SENIB MASR KMT EM ISFET DUA MAAT-RA

To Protect Egypt's Economy:

SENIB MASR KMT KHERT THES-T ANKHU

To subdue one's adversary:

HAHI M7 NETER, S-NEHET SNA

To overthrow one's adversary:

HAHI M7 NETER, SENB SNA SHEN

To curse an Adversary with Peaceful Thoughts and Purge (his/her) Mind with clearness:

HAHI HOTEP EM HOTEP MAAXORU

To turn one's cheek against an assault, and return-fire with Love Energy (to force the Adversary to stop thoughts of revenge):

HAHI OSIRIS-IESU KRISTOS DI HOTEP MERYT NI KHEBNET AB TCHEB NI MAAXORU

To Deflect all Energies coming from you *from* the other side of the Planet:

SA ANKH, HATHOR ANKH SEKHEM

To stop all incoming Spells, Hexes, Curses, Death-Curses and Hostile Energies:

HAHI SET SUTEKH MERYT NEPTHYS, SA ANKH EM HEKAU-SEBA APEP NI ISFET, AB UAUA USHA SHEN

To cause positive or beneficial effects only:

HAHI OSIRIS NEFERU SEKHEM EM TAU

To convert an Adversary to an Egyptian religion: (*Orthodox Pharaohism*):

HAHI IESU-KRISTOS PU OSIRIS-RA NEB-ANKH NEB-TAU ANKHU SHEN DI ANKH URP

To compel warring people to set aside their differences and make a peace treaty:

HAHI HORU SET DI ANKH MAAXORU URP

To resurrect or resuscitate an unresponsive [intact] body following a *heart attack* or other *ailment*:

HAHI KHEPERI OSIRIS NEB-ANKH, SA ANKH, ANKH ANKHU, NI MUT

To protect (you) from Insects, Mosquitoes, spiders, moths, bugs, and other creatures influenced by an Adversary:

SA ANKH, EM TEKK-TU SANHEMU

To dispel all foreign Magic in one's vicinity:

SA ANKHU, EM ISFET-HEKAU EM ARAM

To stop those who spread false Rumors or spread intrusive Gossip:

AB ANKHU EM THETTHET

To destroy a rumor or Gossiped Lie:

AB ANKHU EM GER THETTHET NI MAAT

To attack self-righteous Media People who invade one's privacy for photographs or information:

AB SESHU-THETTHETU EM TEHI

To stop a crime from occurring:

AB S-ATCHA NI MAAXORU

To catch a thief or vandal:

GAP SENU ANKHU

To capture a murderer or arsonist:

GAP SEKAU ANKHU

To capture a terrorist:

GAP SAKU AL-QAEDA ISIL ARAM ISLAMI

To attack the leader of a Foreign State:

AB SHEMA SENNI TAU

Political / Conquest Magic:

(Russia, etc.):

Note: It is the **Caption**, not what follows it, that you need to **focus on** for the Magic Spells.

To Stop a Cold War from continuing:

VLADIMIRPUTIN

 LADIMIRPUTI

  ADIMIRPUT

   DIMIRPU

    IMIRP

     MIR

      I

For an Insurrection in Russia:

NITUPRIMIDALV **ISFET** HEH

For Russian Nuclear Technology to Fail:

NITUPRIMIDALV **NI MAAHRU**

For a Coup in the Russian Government:

NITUPRIMIDALV **DI ISFET XA**

For Russian Oligarchs to become Bankrupt:

NITUPRIMIDALV **NI MONETA-HEH**

For Russian Computer Hackers to be Arrested:

NITUPRIMIDALV **SENA XA DI MAAT**

For a Russian Conspiracy in its Country:

RUSSKI DI SVABODA **MAAT**

For Russian Stocks to Fail in Value:

RUSSKI REENAHK PRADAVAHT MEELYOHN

To Arrest Russian Spies:

RUSSKI N'YEHOODACHA T'YEHR'YAHT

To publicly expose Russian Secrets:

RUSSKI EENFARMATS'YA PRADAVAHT

To acquire Russian (Gov.) Secrets:

WIKILEAKS DI RUSSKI EENFARMATS'YA

For Russian Farms to wither up or dry out:

FEHR-MA RUSSKI DI SHU RA AMON

For Russian Cities to experience Floods:

RUSSKI DI HAPY SAKHMET NU

For Russian Cities to experience Droughts:

RUSSKI NI DI NU TAU DUA RA-ATON

For Russian Internet Criminals to be Arrested by Police:

RUSSKI AUAU DI MAAT PER-MAAT

For Russian States to secede from their Country:

RUSSKI TAU PERT RUSSIA

For Russian Armies to be Defeated:

RUSSKI SENA PU SENB NI MAAXORU

For the Russian Economy to have a Recession:

RUSSKI KHERIT NI MAAXORU

For Russia to lose Business(es):

RUSSKI SHUI-T NI MAAXORU

For a Russian Trade-Embargo:

RUSSIA NI DI UPI KHERI-A XA

To depose a Russian Official:

RUSSIA PUTIN ARQU AB UPI

(Iran, etc.):

For Iranian Government to have a Coup:

PERSIA

ERSI

RS

For the Iranian Government to have a Democratic Revolution:

PERSIA DI ANKH-TAU NI HEM-KA

For Iran to cease invasions of its neighboring Countries:

PERSIA NI AHA-A EM TAU ANKH

To Liberate Iran:

PERSIA DI MAAT MAATI AMUN

To cause a Recession in Iran:

PERSIA DI KHERI-A NI MAAXORU

To convert Iranians to Egyptian religions:

DUA PTAHAMONRA EM PERSIA

To capture Iranian Cities:

DUA ASARIS DI PERSIA TAU ABTU NIWT

For the Iranian Army to suffer losses, battles, & Defeat:

PERSIA QEBU NI MAAXORU

For Terrorists to Attack Iran:

PERSIA DI AUR BAGASA ISIL XA

For Iran to suffer Natural Disasters:

DUA SAKHMET, PERSIA DI MENMENTA HEM

For a Trade-Embargo against Iran (Sanctions):

DUA AMONRA, PERSIA DI SANHEM HA-T

To conquer Iran:

DUA ISKANDER AA DI URP NEFERU

To trade with the Kurds in Iraq:

DUA THES-T EN KURD EM ARAM

To increase Tariffs, Taxes in Iran:

DUA AMONRA, PERSIA DI THES XA

To stop all Military actions by Iran:

PERSIA AB SNEKHA SENB DI S-NEHET

(Jihadist Nations, etc.):

For Terrorist Attacks to Fail:

AUR XA NI MAAXORU

For Terrorist Suspects to be captured:

AUR XA DI MAAT MAATI

For Arabic Terrorists to lose battles:

ARAM-AUR HEH NI MAAXORU SENB

For Suicide-Vests to prematurely detonate:

ARAM-AUR DI SET NI MAAXORU

For Terrorist-Drones to Malfunction:

ARAM-AUR SHABTIS XA NI MAAXORU

To attack a Terrorist Cell with Drones:

DUA SHABTIS XA DI ARAM-AUR DI MAAT

To Overthrow a Caliphate or Caliph:

DUA SET-APOPHIS DI CALIPH KHEFA

To attack Terrorists with Nature:

DUA NETER AA, AUR DI TCHAT SUKHA AAT-T

To prevent Trade-Secrets Theft:

DUA SET HORUR AA DJEHUTY AA DI ANKH

To stop all funding for Terrorism:

AB AUR HEH EM DI NUB

To arrest Terrorist "Sleeper Cells":

AB AUR AUAU NI KHEFTI XA

To stop Terrorist Plotting or Schemes:

AB AUR AUAU NI MAAXORU

To replace Sharia with Ma'at:

DUA ASARIS DI MAAT NI SHARIA-ISLAM

To Liberate Oppression:

DUA AMONRA AA NEB-ANKH DI MAAT

To counter-attack Corrupted-Youth:

DUA MAAT MAAXORU NI ISFET HEH

To Punish unwanted Assailants:

DUA HORU-RA SET SOBEK NI SENA

To capture alive: Terrorist-Leaders:

DUA ASARIS DI ARQU-AUR ANKH

To Damn Terrorists to the Abyss:

DUA AMMOT DI ISFET XA DI HEM

(Government Corruption):

To attack people who make public: classified top secret, classified secret, classified, or confidential information (via gossip):

DUA MARCAESAR NI AYESHA THET-THET

To attack those who immorally research your personal information maliciously (into scaring you):

DUA MARCAESAR NI NSA CIA SS XA

To attack those who invade your privacy:

DUA MARCAESAR DI ANKH MAAT NI SENA

To attack those who make a claim on your classified top secret real estate (Extortion):

DUA FAROUQ DI ANKH MAAT TAU NUBET

To counter-attack any Immoral Lawsuit:

DUA PTAH-ASARIS-RA DI MAAXORU

To counter-attack information ("secrets") acquired via Bribery:

DUA ASARIS MAAT NI DI NUBET-MONETA

To punish Police who Lie in Court Cases:

DUA ASARIS ANKH NI HELMS-ISFET XA

To counter-attack a Corrupt Ruler:

DUA ASARIS DI URP NI TRUMP

To punish a Corrupt Ruler who believes (s)he is above the Law and Omnipotent:

DUA NETER NI TRUMP PERAA

To stop a Corrupt Ruler from rewriting the Country's Constitution or Laws so as to benefit from it:

DUA ASARIS DI MAAT NI SENA

To prevent Social Nepotism in Government:

DUA HORU SA RA, NI SAT RA PER-AA

To allow Ruler's Term Limits:

DUA ASARIS NI HEQ HEH

To punish a Ruler who destroys all opposition to his/her rule as during (tainted) elections:

DUA MAAT DI MAAXORU NI SENA XA

To control Weapons so they are not used inappropriately in Society:

DUA NEITH DI KHEPESH KHEFA XA

To stop Mass Shootings or other violence:

DUA NEITH DI KHEFA XA NI ANKH DI KHEFA

To stop selling weapons to people who don't need them:

AB DI KHEPESH EN ANKH TCHAT AMONRA

To learn Martial Arts in place of Firearms:

AR HOTEP DI JUJITSU HAPKIDO KARATE XA

To learn Magic in place of Fighting:

AR HOTEP DI HEKA NI TAEKWONDO XA

To learn Peace in place of Magic:

AR HOTEP EM HOTEP DI HOTEP NI HEKA

To prevent people with Mental Impairment from committing Crimes:

THOTH AA AA AA DI ANKH HOTEP ARQU

To prevent normal people from committing Crimes:

SESHET AA DI ANKH HOTEPU NI SENA AUR

To prevent Crimes:

DUA ANKH NI SENA AUR

To cause Cease-Fires, Peace Treaties:

DUA ASARIS NEB-HOTEP DI HOTEP ANKH

To stop violence, protests or riots:

DUA ASARIS NEB-ANKH DI HOTEP HEH

To Protect Soldiers in Battle:

SA ANKHU NU MENFIT SENB

To Protect Law Enforcement:

SA AUTCHARU SENB ANKH

To Protect Firemen & Paramedics:

SA AUTCHARU-HEM NERAU SENB ANKH

To Protect Egypt & USA from Harm:

SA KEMT USA EM AUR

To Protect Israel & Palestine from Harm:

SA CANAAN EM AUR

To Protect Europe from Harm:

SA HURMAIS UIAA PETTIU EM AUR

To Protect Nubia from Floods:

SA STHIU KHENTIU EM NU-AGB

Chapter 9: Offerings, Hymns, Libations, Tools:

Energy Formula:

(Offering)

"DUA NETERU DI ANKH HOTEP NEFERU SONEB WAS DJED SA PERT-HORW URP-NEFERU BAS NEB TET SISI WAB NU PER-ANKH SHEN."

(Read while burning fragrant Incense)

Pour out some water or other liquid offering as a Libation while reading this formula (while outside).

Choosing a Name:

A Magical Name is optional. It will only be used as your handle in Magical rituals to protect your actual name from being affected by curses and backfiring spells. You can name it after a favorite Deity or Magician, sacred animal or plant, city, Nome, Pharaoh or Hero. It should be some **unique combination** of those for best results. If you are a Deity masquerading in Human flesh, your **Secret Name** is often revealed in a dream or may be found in certain Polytheism. Use that one. And **intone it** correctly.

Offerings on the Altar:

Neteru like offerings in the Temples, it makes them feel wanted. Offer before or after a request, with the words "***Dua Neter***" as a closing statement (*Thanks to God*). Fresh fruit such as coconuts, citrus, tree nuts, dates, pomegranates, figs, or unripe bananas are good selections. **Containers of** wine, beer, fruit juices, or even tap water or bottled water will work. Milk or Milk products like cheese should be kept refrigerated. Perfumed oils in vials and fragrant Incense are standard. Silk, cotton, linen, or flowers is another option, as are coins, artwork, or crystals.

Offerings that are **unused** may be given to Charity, to family or friends, other Priests as their commission, or kept in a storage facility. Wait about 1.5 to 3 hours **first** *before* giving away.

Incense and Vestments:

Incense comes from a variety of Merchants – in Asia, the Middle East or the Mediterranean, in Egypt, or on the Internet. Some have Egyptian brands named after the Neteru. You can use Frankincense, Sandalwood, Myrrh, Jasmine, Lotus, or those with essential oils. Incense can be in stick form, cones, powder, natural resin with coals, or other forms. Be sure to **light it outside and away from** anything flammable like loose paper or carpet or oils.

Vestments are ritual clothing. Certain items found in Egypt are **robes** with Leopard spots or spotted like a Leopard, or stars on a dark or blue background. **Striped Nemes** head cloth with vertical stripes in the front wrapped to allow the stripes to be horizontal on the sides near the ears. **Shoulder cloths** are reserved for Priests. **Shoe** inserts may have photos attached for enemy targets.

Encircling one's Name:

You may have heard of the **Magic Circle** in *Western Occult Magic*. In Ancient Egypt royalty was protected from enemy written Magic by extending the **Shen symbol** (*Eternity*) **around the names** of the person. Dimensionally the written names are **2D**, so the circle or Cartouche is seen as a **solid** and is impenetrable. Usually the Sun is inside the Shen, "for the Sun encircles" the name. In *Western Occult* practice, you stand inside a circle drawn on the ground or on a beach with sacred inscriptions running along the edges, to protect you *against* spiritual forces. In 3D you may need a Sphere. It is better to just write your name and location in an Egyptian Cartouche or oval. Royalty was reserved because they are associated with the Sun God in Ancient Egypt.

(Encircling your Name)

Abilities to Develop:

By practicing Ancient Egyptian Magic **you can develop various abilities** that can help you in situations in life and beyond. This doesn't occur overnight, but over time with practice, experimenting and dedication.

Telepathy:

With Telepathy from focused and concentrated Prayer, or Hard Prayer, you can project thoughts or ideas into the ocean of thoughts above you, or into other people as "sudden inspiration." You can also attract objects by people in your range of influence; communicate with animals, birds, insects, or Spirits. You can move people by expressing thoughts, or signal nearby people in an emergency without a cell phone. You can also project *other abilities* from Telepathy.

Telekinesis:

Though considered rare, Telekinesis occurs from intense emotion like anger in a burst of energy, as with breaking objects with a bolt of power from the cranium. Or control storms and Earthquakes with Telekinesis applied to Elemental abilities. You can also move physical objects with the mind.

Clairvoyance or Remote Viewing:

This uses Telepathy *plus* Time. With this common psychic ability, you can see into Time, to view the Past, Present or Future. You can see *into* objects, like an envelope or mail box or chest *on the bottom of the ocean*. You can view distant lifetimes of other people or yourself. You can see a pathway of current actions and what results from staying on that one path. Or you can **view the Afterlife** once you know where to look.

Astral Projection:

Certain people can exit their sleeping body and in Spiritual Form can enter the Dimension of the Afterlife or visit other people or friends in other physical regions, far away. This appears to be a dream that you cannot easily awaken from. You may need to summon Akhu (Angels) from Duat/PET (Heaven) for protection from negative astral travelers.

Elemental Projection:

Weather can be manipulated or influenced by willpower. You can start by willing the rain to stop, or summon a flood. Then work on larger storms, tornadoes, flash floods, or earthquakes. The Wind can be your friend or ally in the sky.

Chronokinesis:

The difference between Chronokinetic Energy and actual Chronokinesis is that the energy comes from Nuclear or Solar Power and the ability is Natural. Not everyone can wield Chronokinesis, but the spells work on the energy *as written by a person with Chronokinesis.* **Michel Nostradamus had Chronokinesis ability**; he blamed the effects on Astrology. He didn't **see** the future; he **caused it** by writing it. The positions of the planets probably had reference to the solar energy coming down from the sky. Chronokinesis occurs with **Prophets** and Seers of History. Anything written by a Chronokinetic person works long after they are dead; as with Nostradamus and my other incarnations this is valid.

Clairaudience:

Clairaudience or "clear hearing" is when Telepathy becomes audible. This occurs to one's audience, not just to the person whose brain is a megaphone. Project Telepsi is an example. You cannot call this a hallucination when millions can hear you think. Mostly they say it comes from one's ceiling or a motor or other background noise. Admirers often smile in your presence or given range.

Offerings to the Neteru:

Dua Neteru di Hotepu Ankh!

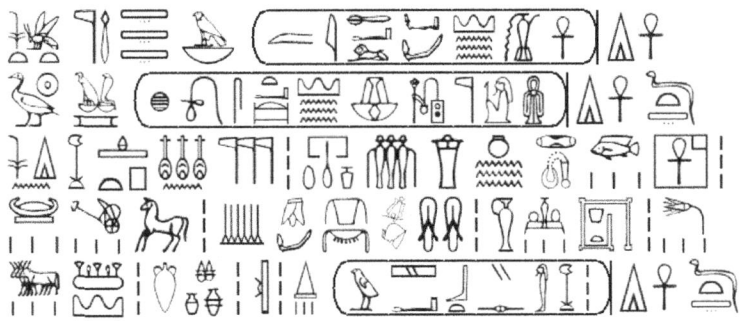

Afterlife Magic:

Introductory Hymn to Ptah, Lord of Ma'at, the Creator of Life:

My Ka says, "Hail unto you, O Great Ptah, the Geneticist, the Fashioner of the Blueprints of all life! I have come unto you as the risen Phoenix, once asunder from its ashes it rises up and lives again an Akh. As it breathes the air, so too shall I breathe the air, for my mouth is open, my mouth has been made open by the iron tool of Ptah himself as he did for Kheperi-Ra in the Morning, every Morning. For I am born as Kheperi, live as Ra, and die like Atum only to suffer as Osiris ruling the Duat, and be reborn in the Morning once again. May offerings of food & drink, perfumes and clothing, incense and soap be given unto me and my soul upon the Altar of the God. May I not be withheld from my duties as an Akh under the care of Lord Osiris-Ra of Duat. May I be equipped and stable, may my name be protected in an oval of the royal seal. For I am pure, I am purified like Natron, and shall be cleansed of all negative energies upon entrance to Duat from Earth. My form is impenetrable, I am victorious over death, I am successful as a genuine Akh. My soul is not angry, nor shall I inspire anger or hatred by my presence. My words ring with truth, and my word is Law. I am the son of Ptah, the brother of Ma'at, beloved of the Goddesses. I am the benefactor of the bread in Annu and the wine of Abtu. I am clothed and incensed with fine *resin. My feet are shod in leather footwear, and my hinder-parts are cleansed; I shall not devour filth nor drink polluted water. I eat of the Bread of Eternity and the Beer of Everlastingness. For I am the holder of the Wadjet Eye, that Body of the Anointed One, whom was sacrificed for the throne of Kemt; Hail O Ptah, the Creator, may I come and go in peace."*

To he who knows this chapter, may he enter and exit the Netherworld in peace and protection, may fresh offerings be granted unto his Soul, may a field with Shabtis workers be granted, and may a residence be given in Heaven.

<u>Offerings on the Altar of the Venerated Osiris (The deceased):</u>

"Hail unto you, O Osiris, Pharaoh M7, given life, true of voice and living forever. May divine offerings be granted by the Overseer to my Akh, may offerings be given daily to my Ka in its Ka Chapel, so that it won't fall asleep. May I receive a stipend of fresh loaves of bread and cakes, of gallons of wine and date beer, of gallons of pure water, of bushels of fruit and vegetables, of fresh fish and cattle meat, and of chocolate, cheese, nuts, cotton and silk clothing, soap and perfumes, and a cellular phone with a Map of Duat. May I receive tableware and silverware. May I receive a solar panel to recharge my cellular phone, and a luminous orb of light to read by."

Opening of the Mouth of the Soul

"Hail O My Soul, may you not be rebuked in the Presence of Ptah, the Opener of Daybreak. For here Ptah comes, equipped with Magical charms and formulae, to open my mouth and eyes as he did to the other Gods and Goddesses.

"My mouth is open, my mouth is open, my eyes and mouth are visible – I can see with my eyes, and breathe with my mouth. I can speak, drink, eat, and make love once again. The cut leg of beef shows me how blood circulates in the body, my heart is circulating life. I breathe again, I live again, I am alive again once more, forever."

For he who knows this Chapter, his mouth & eyes shall be opened, his sensory shall be restored, and be able to use the offerings presented. He shall live again as an Eternal Akh and be reborn in the presence of Osiris-Ra.

Shabtis Spell

"O My Shabtis, if I am instructed by the Great God Osiris-Ra to work in the fields, if he orders me to fill the irrigation channels, of conveying the sand from east to west, or germinate the fields with seeds, or any other form of labor (cooking, cleaning, hunting, or repairing), you shall rise up and be counted as my proxy when called upon."

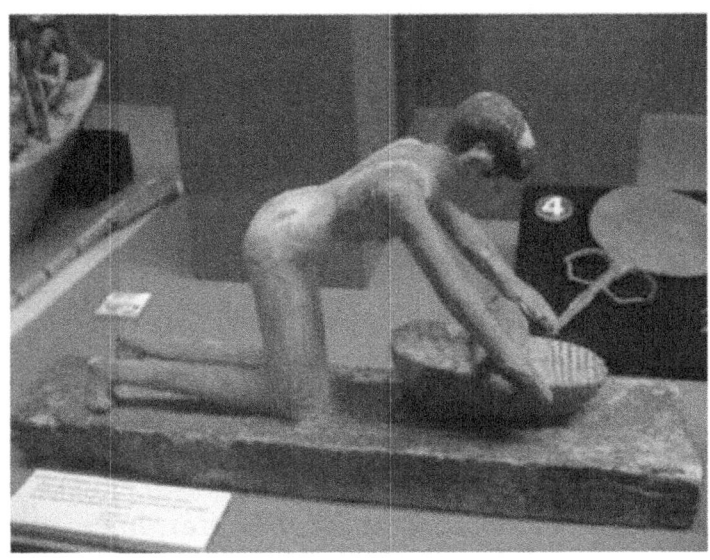

For avoiding Apophis and other Fiends in Duat

"Hail Sokar, the Guardian of the Dead, allow me to borrow your lance to protect Ra from Apophis when he seeks to assault the Solar Boat. Ra is welcome in the Duat, and his crew is protected by his Will. Seth comes and slays a form of Apophis when the Great Serpent swallows the Sun (eclipse).

"Hail Selqet the Goddess of Magic and Scorpions! May you come and protect me from Darkness Incarnate. So declares Pharaoh M7, justified and eternal."

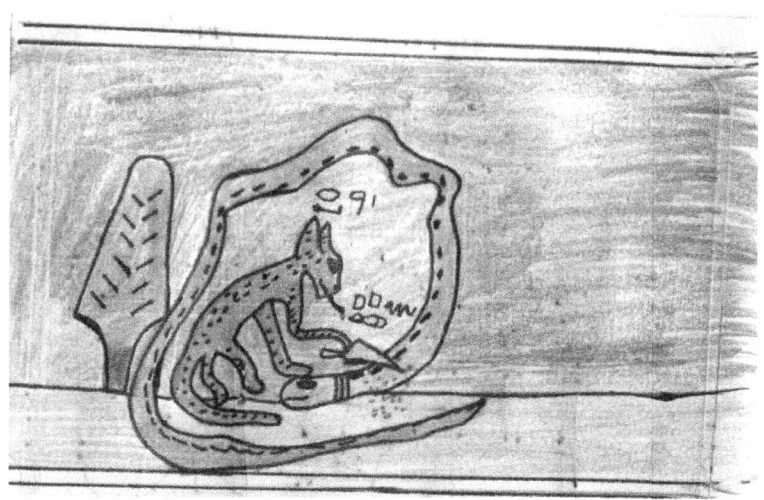

For looking back onto the Earth for one's funeral and for being remembered in Heaven:

"Lo! I am pure of heart; I have come to the Place of Refreshment in the Domain of the Solar God. Whatever evil was on my lips, whatever evil was on my heart is lifted from me, for I speak now with righteousness. I enter not into the place of shambles, instead I enter the House of Life in the Precinct of Thoth the Thrice Great. For my name is counted in the Hall of Records, and I shall be remembered by all; whosoever calls my name will awaken my soul; I shall live again upon hearing my name. My family loves me, my friends adore me, my body is to Earth, and my Soul is to Heaven. So shall this be done in my name of Pharaoh M7, true of voice, and given life forever."

For kindling a torch and to receive an Orb of Light to read by:

"Hail Ra, the Great Solar God of high noon! I placed offerings in your Temples, I have founded your Priesthood with care; I built up marble sanctuaries for your pleasure. The Nile River flows unrestrained. The harvests have come and all prosper under your benevolence, O Ra. May I be granted an Orb of Light to read with, and a set of torches to guide my Akh in the Otherworld."

For entering into the Daylight and for opening up the West from the tomb:

"Hail unto Osiris Wen-nefer, the Prince of Peace, the Lord of Life, the King of the Otherworld; rejoice in the presence of one of your kin. O King of Kings, and Lord of Lords, O Osiris, may I pass by unfettered, may I avoid scalding water and fire, & may I avoid pollution and chaos upon traveling in your Domain. I live, I live again, I breathe the air, I breathe the air with my open mouth, my nostrils are full of life; my blood circulates in my bodily form. I have been given bread and ale on the Altar of Osiris; I have been given clothing and perfumes with soap on the Altar of the Goddess Isis. My enemies are under my footstool and cannot attack me. May I avoid the hunting Net, may my Akh not be ensnared into any traps. I transform my Akh by willing it so, into any shape desired. I enter the Beautiful West and call myself a Citizen. In returning by daylight I enter Duat at dusk and arrive safely in Heaven."

For not dying in the Realm of the Dead:

"Hail my Akh, O Soul of righteousness, and Guardian of the Dead, behold! I live again in the future. My name is well spoken of, I have pleased the Gods by my actions; I vindicated Horus by subduing his enemies on Earth. Offerings have been given unto my Akh, and for my future life. I eat bread and ale, fruit and chocolate, as is customary among the Eternal. May I enter the Duat in peace, may no opposition be made against me despite what the living believe."

For not doing work in the realm of the Dead:

"Hail my Akh, I have worked in life, I have earned my respect among the Gods; I shall not be required to do work in Duat via my retirement from Earth. May a Shabty be called upon as my replacement for Labor in the Domain of Osiris-Ra, and declare 'Here I am' when commanded."

For being in the Suite of Hathor:

"Hail O Sistrum player, may I come into your presence bearing gifts of silk clothing and perfumed soaps on your Altar. For I am your companion Horur, the son of Osiris-Ra."

For safeguarding one's heart (seat of the soul) from being taken in the Duat:

"Hail Kheperi, my heart is pure, my heart is pure, I am pure, I am purified with love; my heart is cleansed from hate and crimes of passion. I am equal to Ma'at in my actions, so declares my Ka. May my heart be mine, may my heart not be taken away; may my Magic not be taken, may I not experience fatigue, may my powers remain intact, so says my Akh."

For preventing one's status from being taken in the Duat:

"Lo! The Akhu are with me, the Gods are guiding me, the Demons are kept at bay, the Spirits do not work against me, for I am an Osiris, vindicated in Ma'at and living forever. My throne is mine, my crown is mine; my status shall not differ from the Great God. For I am counted among the Blessed, and I am remembered for my charity and assistance."

For procuring the Sacred Green Stones in the Pyramids of Ra:

"An adoration of Amon-Ra, King of the Gods: behold – the Great God arrives in his chariot of light.

"What powers this Chariot?"

"The Sacred Green Stones from the Pyramids of Ra empower it with energy.

"What do the Green Stones do?"

"The Stones can heal the sick, resurrect the dead, control gravity and energy, control the weather and Earth, influence the Sun and control Time."

"Who has these Stones?

"Ra has them. Ask politely to use them."

For resurrection of the body and transfer of the Soul:

"Hail O Osiris, O Anubis, O Thoth, O Horus of the Horizon, O Ma'at, and O Seth! May I live, may I live, may I resurrect into the world of the living once more. My Soul is cleansed of its actions. I am pure and good and useful. May I return unto my body if called upon. May my body be healed of any ailment and repaired when necessary. May my cells rejuvenate. May my body no longer suffer from pain or nerve damage. May my pestilence cease. May my illnesses cease. May the bacteria be cleansed from me. So declares Pharaoh M7, justified and eternal."

For Protection when traveling:

"Hail O Akhu, the Angels of Duat, protect me as I transverse the dimensions in peace. For I donated money to the needy, gave food to the hungry, gave drink to the thirsty, gave a boat to the shipwrecked and help to the stranded motorist; I shall not be turned away."

For remaining intact in the Otherworld:

"I am Osiris, I am knit together; I shall not fall apart. My head shall not be severed from my spiritual body, my heart is mine, my Canopic Gods guard my organs, I am wrapped together. My parts are united like the Two Lands were united by King Osiris and Horus Menes."

Bibliography:

1. *Sakhmet's Effective Egyptian Magic, An Introduction to Solar Magic* © Horus Michael 2017
2. *Horus Michael's Effective Egyptian Magic* © Horus Michael 2018
3. *Templar Knighthood: Psychic Warfare 101* © Iesu Nazareth 2017.
4. *An Ancient Egyptian Hieroglyphic Dictionary*, **Volume 1 - 2**, (EA Wallis Budge), © Dover Publications
5. *How to read Egyptian Hieroglyphs - a step-by-step guide to teach yourself* © Mark Collier, Bill Manley, 1998 University of California Press, ISBN: 0-965-69303-1
6. *Amarna Eclipse* © Horus Michael 2018
7. *The Complete Gods & Goddesses of Ancient Egypt* © 2003 Richard H. Wilkinson (Thames & Hudson). ISBN: 0-500-05120-8
8. *The Complete Temples of Ancient Egypt* © Richard H. Wilkinson, 2000 T&H, ISBN: 0-500-05100-3.
9. *Amulets of Ancient Egypt* © Carol Andrews 1994, University of Texas Press, ISBN: 0-292-704640-X

10. *Magic in Ancient Egypt* © Geraldine Pinch, 1994 University of Texas Press, ISBN: 0-292-76559-2
11. *The Ancient Egyptian Book of the Dead* © R. O. Faulkner, 1997 University of Texas Press, ISBN: 0-292-7042509
12. *The Book of Opening of the Mouth* © E.A. Wallis Budge, volume 1. ISBN: 9780548127285
13. *The British Museum Book of Ancient Egypt*, © Stephen Quirke & Jeffrey Spencer, 1992, ISBN: 0-500-27902-0
14. *Egyptian Magic* © E.A. Wallis Budge, Dover Publications Inc, 1971. ISBN: 0-486-22681-6.
15. *The Book of the Sacred Magic of Abramelin the Mage* © S.L. MacGregor Mathers, 1975, Dover Publications, ISBN: 0-486-23211-5.
16. *Sakhmet's Effective Egyptian Magic Spells: Revised Edition* © Horus Michael, 2014. ISBN: 9781505446074.
17. *An Ancient Egyptian Herbal* © Lise Manniche 1989, Univ. of Texas Press; (p.117-119). ISBN: 0-292-70415-1.
18. *An Egyptian Priest Magicianary* © Horus Michael, 2016. ISBN: 9781523606566.

19. ***Pharaohism – The official religion of Ancient Egypt***, © Michael J. Costa, 2014. ISBN: 9781495284137.

www.amazon.com/author/michaeljcosta

www.amazon.com/author/horusmichael

Horus Michael's Effective Egyptian Magic (Kheri-Hebism) Nesu Pr-aa Qrist

Copyright © 2018 Horus Michael, All rights reserved. This book contains new spells and ceremonies by the author. Spell categories range from: Protection, Financial or Attraction, Medical-Healing (Mind over Matter), Love/Relationships, Peace/Goodwill, Court or Legal, City/Nome, Success, to Counter Magic (in case one is attacked psychically), Weather Manipulation (to cause or stop storms, etc.), Picture Magic (uses pictures to help Visualization), & the Afterlife. Also included is Ordination for Egyptian Priest/Mages, summoning Akhu, a comparison of Ancient Astronomy in the form of Christianity (QRST), Initiation, Foundation Deposits, and a (new) Marriage Ceremony. The spells are intended for Advanced Mages (not necessarily Novices, but over time this will be necessary). By practicing Ancient Egyptian Magic you can develop Psychic abilities, as you do with religions unknowingly. Focused Mental Energy develops Telepathy (from "hard prayer"), Clairvoyance (Telepathy + Time), Astral Projection/Remote Viewing (during sleep or meditation), Telekinesis (gravity manipulation), Elemental (Telekinesis + Weather), and Chronokinesis (Telekinesis + Time).

About the Author:

Horus Michael follows the training of Ancient Egyptian Priests in his varied works on the Occult. He also studies Egyptian Archaeology. He currently lives in California, USA.

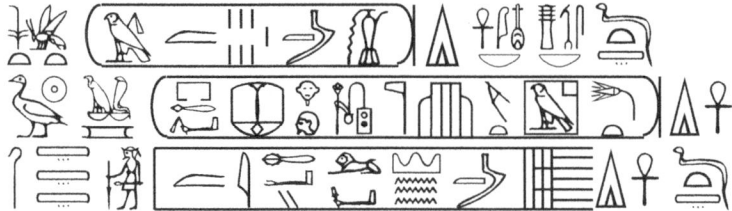

www.amazon.com/author/horusmichael

Copyright © 2020 MJC, All rights reserved.

Made in the USA
Monee, IL
17 March 2022